Spiritual Parenting

Spiritual Parenting

C.H. SPURGEON

 Whitaker House

SPIRITUAL PARENTING

ISBN: 0-88368-265-6
Printed in the United States of America
Copyright © 1995 by Whitaker House

Whitaker House
30 Hunt Valley Circle
New Kensington, PA 15068

    4 5 6 7 8 9 10 11 12 13 14 / 06 05 04 03 02 01 00

Contents

Chapter 1

How to "Feed My Lambs"

Feed My lambs.
—John 21:15

The best of the church are none too good for this work. Do not think because you have other service to do that you should take no interest in this form of holy work, but kindly, according to your opportunities, stand ready to help the little ones, and to cheer those whose chief calling is to attend to them. To all of us, this message comes: *"Feed My lambs."* To the minister and to all who have any knowledge of the things of God the commission is given. See to it that you look after the children that are in Christ Jesus. Peter was a leader among believers, yet he fed the lambs.

Lambs are the young of the flock. So, then, we ought to look especially and carefully after those who are young in grace. They may be old in years, and yet they may be mere babes in grace as to the length of their spiritual life. Therefore, they need to be under a good shepherd. As soon as a person is converted and added to the church, he should become the object of the care and kindness of his fellow members. He has just newly come among us, but has no familiar friends among the saints. Therefore, let us all be friendly to him. We should even take leave of our older comrades as we must be doubly kind towards those who are newly escaped from the world and have come to find a refuge with the Almighty and His people.

Watch with ceaseless care over those newborn babes who are strong in desires, but strong in nothing else. They have but just crept out of darkness, and their eyes can scarcely bear the light. Let us be a shade to them until they grow accustomed to the blaze of gospel sunshine.

Addict yourselves to the holy work of caring for the feeble and despondent. Peter himself that morning must have felt like a newly-enlisted soldier, for he had in a sense ended his public Christian life by denying his Lord, and he had begun it again when he *"went out, and wept bitterly"* (Luke 22:62). He was now making a new confession of his faith before his Lord and his brothers. Therefore, because he was thus made to sympathize with recruits, he is commissioned to act as a guardian to them. Young converts are too timid to ask our help, and so our Lord introduces them to us. With an emphatic word of command, He says, *"Feed My lambs."* This shall be our reward: *"Inasmuch as ye have done it unto one of the least of these my brethren, ye have done it unto Me"* (Matthew 25:40).

However young a believer may be, he should make an open confession of his faith and be enfolded with the rest of the flock of Christ. We are not among those who are suspicious of youthful piety: we could never see more reason for such suspicions in the case of the young than in the case of those who repent late in life. Of the two, we think the latter are more to be questioned than the former: for a selfish fear of punishment and dread of death are more likely to produce a counterfeit faith than mere childishness could.

How much has the child missed which might have spoiled it! How much the child does not know which, thank God, we hope it never does! Oh, how much there is of brightness and trustfulness about children when converted to God which is not seen in older converts! Our Lord Jesus evidently felt deep sympathy with children. The man little resembles Christ who looks upon children as a trouble in the world and treats them as if they must either be little deceivers or foolish simpletons.

To you who teach in our schools is given this joyous privilege of finding out where these young disciples are who are truly the lambs of Christ's flock. To you He says, *"Feed My lambs."* That means, instruct such as are truly gracious, but young in years.

It is very remarkable that the word used here for *"feed My lambs"* is very different from the word employed in the precept, *"feed My sheep"* (John 21:16). I will not trouble you with Greek words, but the second *"feed"* means exercise the office of a shepherd, rule, regulate, lead, manage them, do all that a shepherd has to do toward a flock. However, this first *"feed"* does not include all that. It means distinctively, feed. It directs teachers to a duty which they may, perhaps, neglect—namely, that of instructing children in the faith. The lambs do not need as much keeping in order as we do who know so much, and yet know so little, who think we are so far advanced that we judge one another and contend and emulate. Christian children mainly need to be taught the doctrine, precept, and life of the Gospel: they require to have divine truth put before them clearly and forcibly. Why should higher doctrines, those of grace, be kept back from them? They are not as some say, bones; or if they are bones, they are full of marrow and covered with fatness.

If there is any doctrine too difficult for a child, it is the fault of the teacher's conception of it than of the child's power to receive it, provided that the child is really converted to God. It is ours to make doctrine simple; this is to be a main part of our work. Teach the little ones the whole truth and nothing but the truth, for instruction is the great need of the child's nature.

A child has not only to live as you and I have, but also to grow. Hence, he has double need of food. When fathers say of their boys, "What appetites they have!" they should remember that we also would have great appetites if we had not only to keep the machinery going, but to enlarge it at the same time. Children in grace have to grow, rising to greater capacity in knowing, being, doing, and feeling, and to greater power from God.

Thus, above all children must be fed. They must be well-fed, or instructed, because they are in danger of having their cravings perversely satisfied with error. **Youth is susceptible to evil doctrine**. Whether we teach young Christians truth or not, the devil will be sure to teach them error. They will hear of it somehow, even if they are watched by the most careful guardians. The only way to keep chaff out of the child's cup is to fill it brimful with good wheat. Oh, that the Spirit of God may help us do this! The more the young are taught, the better; it will keep them from being misled.

We are especially exhorted to feed them because they are so **likely to be overlooked**. I am afraid our sermons often go over the heads of the younger folk—who, nevertheless, may be as true Christians as the older ones. Blessed is he who can so speak as to be understood by a child! Blessed is that godly woman who in her class so adapts herself to girlish modes of thought that the truth from her heart streams into the children's hearts without obstruction or hindrance.

We are especially exhorted to feed the young because this work is so **profitable**. Do what we may with persons converted late in life, we can never make much of them. We are very glad of them for their own sakes. But at seventy, what remains, even if they live another ten years? Train up a child, and he may have fifty years of holy service before him. We are glad to welcome those who come into the vineyard at the eleventh hour, but they have hardly taken up their pruning hook and their spade before the sun goes down and their short day's work is ended. The time spent in training the late convert is greater than the space reserved for his actual service.

On the other hand, take a child convert and teach him well. Just as young piety often becomes eminent piety, that distinguished piety may have a stretch of years of service in which God may be glorified and others may be blessed. Thus, such work is profitable in a high degree.

It is also most beneficial work to ourselves. It exercises our humility and helps to keep us lowly and meek. It also trains our patience. Let those who doubt this try it, for even young Christians exercise the patience of those who believe in them, and who are therefore anxious that their young charges should justify their confidence in them. If you want big-souled, large-hearted men or women, look for them among those who are much engaged among the young, bearing with their follies, and sympathizing with their weaknesses for Jesus' sake.

Chapter 2

Do Not Hinder the Children

*But Jesus said, Suffer little children,
and forbid them not, to come unto me: for of
such is the kingdom of heaven.
—Matthew 19:14*

Concerning this hindering of children, let us watch its action. I think the results of this sad feeling about children coming to the Savior is to be seen, first, in the fact that often there is nothing in our services for the children. The sermon is over their heads, and the preacher does not think that this is any fault; in fact, he rather rejoices that it is so.

Some time ago, a person who wanted, I suppose, to make me feel my own insignificance, wrote to say that he had met with a number of people of a certain ethnic background who had read my sermons with evident pleasure. He wrote in a derogatory fashion that he believed my sermons were very suitable for this group. Yes, my preaching was just the right sort of stuff for them. The gentleman did not dream what sincere pleasure he caused me: for if I am understood by poor people, by servant girls, by children, I am sure I can be understood by others. I am ambitious to preach for all people, especially the simple, the rag-tag, the castoffs. I think nothing greater than to win the hearts of the lowly.

So, too, is it with regard to children. People occasionally say of such a one, "He is only fit to teach children; he is no preacher." I tell you, in God's sight, he is no preacher who does not care for the children. There should be at least a part of every sermon and service that will suit the little ones. It is an error which permits us to forget this.

Parents sin in the same way when they omit religion from the education of their children. Perhaps the thought is that their children cannot be converted while they are children, and so it is of small consequence where they go to school in their tender years. Not so!

Many parents even forget this when their girls and boys are ending their school days. They send them away to the Continent, to places foul with every moral and spiritual danger, with the idea that there they can complete an elegant education. In how many cases I have seen that education completed, and it has produced young men who are fast-paced profligates, and young women who are mere flirts. *"Whatsoever a man soweth, that shall he also reap"* (Galatians 6:7).

Let us expect our children to know the Lord. Let us from the beginning mingle the name of Jesus with their *ABC*'s. Let them read their first lessons from the Bible. Remarkably, there is no book from which children learn to read so quickly as from the New Testament: there is a charm about that book which draws forth the infant mind. But let us never be guilty, as parents, of forgetting the religious training of our children. If we do, we may be guilty of the blood of their souls.

Another result is that **the conversion of children is not expected** in many of our churches and congregations. I mean, that they do not expect the children to be converted as children. The theory is that if we can impress youthful minds with principles which may, in after years, prove useful to them, we have done a great deal. But to convert children as children, and to regard them as being as much believers as their seniors, is regarded as absurd. To this supposed absurdity, I cling with all my heart. I believe that of children is the kingdom of God, both on earth and in heaven.

Another bad result is that **the conversion of children is not believed**. Certain suspicious people always file their teeth a bit when they hear of a newly-converted child: they will have a bite at him if they can. They very rightly insist that these children should be carefully examined before they are baptized and admitted into the church. However, they are wrong in insisting that only in exceptional instances are they to be received. We quite agree with them as to the care to be exercised, but it should be the same in all cases, and neither more nor less in the cases of children.

How often do people expect to see in boys and girls the same **solemnity of behavior** which is seen in older people! It would be a good thing for us all if we had never stopped being boys and girls, but had added to all the excellencies of a child the virtues of a man. Surely, it is not necessary to kill the child to make the saint? It is thought by the more severe that a converted child must become twenty years older in a minute.

A very solemn person once called me from the playground after I had joined the church and warned me of the impropriety of playing at trap, bat, and ball with the boys. He said, "How can you play like others, if you are a child of God?" I answered that I was employed as an usher, and it was part of my duty to join in the amusements of the boys. My venerable critic thought that this altered the matter very materially. But it was clearly his view that a converted boy, as such, ought never to play!

Do not others **expect from children more perfect conduct** than they themselves exhibit? If a gracious child should lose his temper, or act wrongly in some trifling thing through forgetfulness, straight way he is condemned as a little hypocrite by those who are a long way from being perfect themselves. Jesus says, *"Take heed that ye despise not one of these little ones"* (Matthew 18:10). Take heed that you say not an unkind word against your younger brethren in Christ, your little sisters in the Lord. Jesus sets such great store by His dear lambs, that He carries them in His bosom. I charge you who follow your Lord in all things to show a like tenderness to the little ones of the divine family.

"They brought young children to Him, that He should touch them: and His disciples rebuked those that brought them. But when Jesus saw it He was much displeased" (Mark 10:13-14). He was not often displeased; certainly He was not often *"much displeased."* And when *"He was much displeased,"* we may be sure that the case was serious. He was displeased at these children being pushed away from Him, for it was so contrary to His mind about them.

The disciples did wrong to the mothers. They rebuked the parents for doing a motherly act—doing, in fact, what Jesus loved them to do. They brought their children to Jesus out of respect to Him: they valued a blessing from

18

His hands more than gold. They expected that the benediction of God would go with the touch of the great Prophet. They may have hoped that a touch of the hand of Jesus would make their children's lives bright and happy. Though there may have been a measure of weakness in the parents' thought, yet the Savior could not judge harshly of that which arose out of reverence to His Person. He was therefore much displeased to think that those good women, who meant Him honor, should be roughly repulsed.

There was also wrong done to the children. Sweet little ones! What had they done that they should be chided for coming to Jesus? They had not meant to intrude. Dear things! They would have fallen at His feet in reverent love for the sweet-voiced Teacher, who charmed not only men, but children, by His tender words. The little ones meant no ill, and why should they be blamed?

Besides, there was wrong done to Himself. It might have made men think that Jesus was stiff, reserved, and self-exalted, like the rabbis. If they had thought that He could not condescend to children, they would have sadly slandered the reputation of His great love. His heart was a great harbor where many little ships might cast anchor. Jesus, the child-man, was never more at home than with children. The child Jesus had an affinity for children.

Was He to be represented by His own disciples as shutting the door against the children? It would do a sad injury to His character.

Therefore, grieved at the **triple evil which wounded the mothers, the children, and Himself**, He was sorely displeased. Anything we do to hinder a dear child from coming to Jesus greatly displeases our dear Lord. He cries to us, "Stand off. Let them alone. Let them come to Me, and forbid them not."

Next, it was **contrary to His teaching**. Jesus went on to say, *"Whosoever shall not receive the kingdom of God as a little child, he shall not enter therein"* (Mark 10:15). Christ's teaching was not that there is something in us to fit us for the kingdom, and that a certain number of years may make us capable of receiving grace. His teaching all went the other way—namely, that we are to be nothing, and that the less we are and the weaker we are, the better; for the less we have of self, the more room there is for His divine grace.

Do you think you will come to Jesus up the ladder of knowledge? Come down. You will meet Him at the base. Do you think you may reach Jesus up the steep hill of experience? Come down, dear climber. He stands in the plain. "Oh, but when I am old, I shall then be prepared for Christ." Stay where you are, young man. Jesus meets you at the door of life.

20

You were never more fit to meet Him than just now. He asks nothing of you but that you will be nothing, and that He may be all in all to you. That is His teaching: and to send back the child because it has not this or that is to fly in the teeth of the blessed doctrine of the grace of God.

Once more, it was **quite contrary to Jesus Christ's practice**. He made them see this; for *"He took them up in His arms, put His hands upon them and blessed them"* (Mark 10:16). All His life long there is nothing in Him liko rejection and refusing He said truly, *"Him that cometh to Me, I will in no wise cast out"* (John 6:37). If He did cast out any because they were too young, the text would be falsified at once: but that can never be. He is the receiver of all who come to Him. It is written, *"This Man receiveth sinners, and eateth with them"* (Luke 15:2). All His life, He might be pictured as a shepherd with a lamb in His bosom: never as a cruel shepherd setting his dogs upon the lambs and driving them and their mothers away.

Chapter 3

The Disciples and the Mothers

They brought young children to Him, that He should touch them: and His disciples rebuked those that brought them. But when Jesus saw it He was much displeased.
—Mark 10:13-14

The immediate disciples of our Lord were a highly honorable band of men. Despite their mistakes and shortcomings, they must have been greatly sweetened by living near to one so perfect and so full of love. I gather that if these men, who were the cream of the cream, rebuked the mothers who brought their young children to Christ, it must be a pretty common offense in the church of God.

I fear that the chilling frost of this mistake is felt almost everywhere. I am not going to make any ungenerous statement. However, I think if a little personal investigation were made, many of us might find ourselves guilty on this point and might be led to cry with Pharaoh's butler, *"I do remember my faults this day"* (Genesis 41:9).

Have we laid ourselves out for the conversion of children as much as we have done for the conversion of grown-up folks? What! Do you think me sarcastic? Do you lay yourselves out for anybody's conversion? What must I say to you? It is dreadful that the Cainite spirit should enter a believer's heart and make him say, *"Am I my brother's keeper?"* (Genesis 4:9). It is a shocking thing that we should ourselves eat the fat and drink the sweet, but leave the famishing multitudes to perish. Tell me, if you did care for the salvation of souls, would you not think it rather too commonplace a matter to begin with boys and girls? Your feeling is shared by many. The fault is common.

I believe, however, that this feeling, in the case of the apostles, was caused by zeal for Jesus. These good men thought that the bringing of children to the Savior would cause an interruption: He was engaged in much better work. He had been confounding the Pharisees, instructing the masses, and healing the sick. Could it be right to pester Him with children? The little ones would not understand His teaching, and they did not need His miracles. Why should they be brought in to disturb His great doings?

Therefore, the disciples as good as said, "Take your children back, good women. Teach them the law yourselves, instruct them in the Psalms and the Prophets, and pray with them. Every child cannot have Christ's hands laid on it. If we allow one set of children to come, we shall have all the neighborhood swarming about us, and the Savior's work will be grievously interrupted. Do you not see this? Why do you act so thoughtlessly?" The disciples had such reverence for their Master that they would send the prattlers away, lest the great Rabbi should seem to become a mere teacher of babes. This may have been a zeal for God, but it was not according to knowledge.

Likewise in these days, certain believers would hardly like to receive many children into the church, lest it should become a society of boys and girls. Surely, if these come into the church in any great numbers, the church may be spoken of in terms of reproach! The outside world will call it a mere Sunday school.

I remember that when a fallen woman had been converted in one of our county towns, there was an objection among certain professors to her being received into the church, and certain lewd fellows of the baser sort even went to the extreme of advertising on the walls that the Baptist minister had baptized a harlot. I told my friend that he should regard it as an honor.

24

Even so, if any reproach us with receiving young children into the church, we will wear the reproach as a badge of honor. Holy children cannot possibly do us any harm. God will send us sufficient men of age and experience to steer the church prudently. We will receive none who fail to yield evidence of the new birth, however old they may be; but we will shut out no believers, however young they may be. God forbid that we should condemn our cautious brothers, but at the same time we wish their caution would show itself where it is more required. Jesus will not be dishonored by the children: we have far more cause to fear the adults.

The apostles' rebuke of the children arose in measure from ignorance of the children's need. If any mother in that throng had said, "I must bring my child to the Master, for he is sore afflicted with a devil," neither Peter, nor James, nor John would have demurred for a moment, but would have assisted in bringing the possessed child to the Savior. Or suppose another mother had said, "My child has a pining sickness upon it, it is wasted to skin and bone; permit me to bring my darling, that Jesus may lay His hands upon her." Then the disciples would all have said, "Make way for this woman and her sorrowful burden."

But these little ones with bright eyes, prattling tongues, and leaping limbs, why should they come to Jesus? They forgot that in those children, with all their joy, health, and apparent innocence, there was a great, grievous need for the blessing of a Savior's grace.

If you indulge in the novel idea that your children do not need conversion, that children born of Christian parents are somewhat superior to others and have good within them which only needs development, one great motive for your devout earnestness will be gone. Believe me, your children need the Spirit of God to give them new hearts and right spirits, or else they will go astray as other children do. Remember that however young they are, there is a stone within the youngest breast; and that stone must be taken away or be the ruin of the child. There is a tendency to evil even where as yet it is not developed into act, and that tendency needs to be overcome by the divine power of the Holy Spirit causing the child to be born again.

If only the church of God would banish the old Jewish idea which still has such a hold on us—namely, that natural birth brings with it covenant privileges! Even under the old covenant there were hints that the true seed was not born after the flesh, but after the spirit, as in the case of Ishmael and Isaac, and Esau and Jacob. Will not even the church of God know that *"That which is born of the flesh is flesh; and that which is born of the Spirit is spirit"*

(John 3:6)? *"Who can bring a clean thing out of an unclean?"* (Job 14:4). The natural birth communicates nature's filthiness, but it cannot convey grace. Under the new covenant, we are expressly told that the sons of God are *"born not of blood, nor of the will of the flesh, nor of the will of man, but of God"* (John 1:13). Under the old covenant, which was typical, the birth according to the flesh yielded privilege. but to come at all under the covenant of grace, *"Ye must be born again"* (John 3:7). The first birth brings you nothing but an inheritance with the first Adam; you must be born again to come under the headship of the second Adam.

But someone brings up the verse, *"For the promise is unto you, and to your children"* (Acts 2:39). Never was a more gross piece of duplicity committed under heaven than the quotation of that text as it is usually cited. I have heard it quoted many times to prove a doctrine which is far removed from that which it clearly teaches. If you take one-half of any sentence a man utters and omit the rest, you may make him say the opposite of what he means. What do you think the text really says? *"The promise is unto you, and to your children, and to all that are afar off, even as many as the Lord our God shall call."* This grand, wide statement is the argument on which is founded the exhortation, *"Repent, and be baptized every one of you"* (Acts 2:38). It is not a declaration of privilege special to any one, but a presentation of grace, as much to all who are afar off as to themselves and to their children. Not a word in the New Testament shows that the benefits of divine grace are in any way transmitted by natural descent. They come to *"as many as the Lord our God shall call,"* whether their parents are saints or sinners. How can people have the impudence to tear off half a text to make it teach what is not true?

You must sorrowfully look upon your children as born in sin, *"shapen in iniquity"* (Psalm 51:5), and heirs *"of wrath, even as others"* (Ephesians 2:3). Even though you may yourself belong to a line of saints and trace your pedigree from minister to minister, all eminent in the church of God, yet your children occupy precisely the same position by their birth as other people's children do. They must be redeemed from under the curse of the law by the precious blood of Jesus, and they must receive a new nature by the work of the Holy Ghost. They are favored by being placed under godly training and under the hearing of the Gospel, but their need and their sinfulness are the same as in the rest of the race. If you think of this, you will see the reason why they should be brought to Jesus Christ—a reason why they should be brought as speedily as possible in the arms of your prayer and faith to Him who is able to renew them.

I have sometimes met with a deeper spiritual experience in children of ten and twelve than I have in certain persons of fifty and sixty. It is an old proverb that some children are born with beards. Some boys are little men, and some girls are little old women. You cannot measure the lives of any of us by our ages. I knew a boy who, when he was fifteen, often heard old Christian people say, "The boy is sixty years old: he speaks with such insight into divine truth." I believe that this youth at fifteen did know far more of the things of God and of soul travail, than any around him, whatever their age might be. I cannot tell you why it is, but so I do know it is, that some are old when they are young, and some are very green when they are old; some are wise when you would expect them to be otherwise, and others are very foolish when you might have expected that they had quit their folly.

Talk not of a child's incapacity for repentance! I have known a child weep herself to sleep for months under a crushing sense of sin. If you would know a deep, bitter, and awful fear of the wrath of God, let me tell you what I felt as a boy. If you would know joy in the Lord, many a child has been as full of it as his little heart could hold. If you want to know what faith in Jesus is, you must not look to those who have been bemuddled by the heretical jargon of the times, but to the dear children who have taken Jesus at His word, believed in Him, loved Him, and therefore know and are sure that they are saved.

Capacity for believing lies more in the child than in the man. We grow less rather than more capable of faith: every year brings the unregenerate mind further away from God and makes it less capable of receiving the things of God. No ground is more prepared for the good seed than that which as yet has not been trodden down as the highway, nor has been as yet overgrown with thorns. Not yet has the child learned the deceits of pride, the falsehood of ambition, the delusions of worldliness, the tricks of trade, the equivocation of philosophy; so far, the child has an advantage over the adult. In any case the new birth is the work of the Holy Ghost, and He can as easily work on youth as on age.

Some, too, have hindered the children because they have been forgetful of the child's value. The soul's price does not depend upon its years. "Oh, it is only a child!" "Children are a nuisance." "Children are always getting in the way." This talk is common. God forgive those who despise the little ones! Will you be very angry if I say that a boy is worthier saving than a man?

It is infinite mercy on God's part to save those who are seventy; for what good can they now do with the latter end of their lives? When we get to be fifty or sixty, we are almost worn out. If we have spent all our early days with the devil, what remains for God? But these dear boys and girls, there is something to be made out of them. If now they yield themselves to Christ, they may have a long, happy, and holy life before them in which they may serve God with all their hearts. Who knows what glory God may have through them? Heathen lands may call them blessed. Whole nations may be enlightened by them. If a famous schoolmaster was accustomed to taking his hat off to his students because he did not know whether one of them might become Prime Minister, we may justly look upon converted children, for we do not know how soon they may be among the angels, or how greatly their light may shine among men. Let us estimate children at their true valuation. Then we will not keep them back, but we will be eager to lead them to Jesus at once.

In proportion to our own spirituality of mind, and in proportion to our own child-like-ness of heart, we will be at home with children and will enter into their early fears and hopes, their budding faith, and opening love. Dwelling among young converts, we will seem to be in a garden of flowers, in a vineyard where the tender grapes give a good aroma.

Chapter 4

The Children's Shepherd

So when they had dined, Jesus saith to Simon Peter, Simon, son of Jonas, lovest thou me more than these? He saith unto him, Yea, Lord; thou knowest that I love thee. He saith unto him, Feed my lambs.
—John 21:15

Simon Peter was not a Welshman, but he had a great deal of what we know as Welsh fire in him. He was just the sort of man to interest the young. Children delight to gather round a fire, whether it be on the hearth or in the heart. Certain persons appear to be made of ice, and children speedily shrink away from them. Congregations or classes grow smaller every Sunday when cold-blooded creatures preside over them. But when a man or a woman has a kindly heart, the children seem to gather readily, just as flies in autumn days swarm on a warm, sunny wall. Therefore, Jesus says to **warm-hearted** Simon, *"Feed My lambs."* He is the man for the office.

Simon Peter was, moreover, an **experienced man**. He had known his own weaknesses. He had felt the pangs of conscience. He had sinned much and had been much forgiven, and now he was brought in tender humility to confess the love and loveliness of Jesus. We want experienced men and women to talk to converted children, and to tell them what the Lord has done for them, and what have been their dangers, their sins, their sorrows, and their comforts. The young are glad to hear the story of those who have been further on the road than they have. I may say of experienced saints—their lips keep knowledge. Experience lovingly narrated is suitable food for young believers, instruction such as the Lord is likely to bless to their nourishing in grace.

Simon Peter was now a **greatly indebted man**. He owed much to Jesus Christ, according to that rule of the kingdom: he loves much who has been forgiven much (see Luke 7:47). Oh, you that have never entered upon this service for Christ, and yet might do it well, come forward at once and say, "I have left this work to younger hands, but I will do so no longer. I have experience, and I trust I yet retain a warm heart within my bosom. I will go and join these workers, who are steadily feeding the lambs in the name of the Lord." So far as to the man who is called to feed the lambs.

When the Lord calls a man to a work, He gives him the **preparation** necessary for that work. How was Peter prepared for feeding Christ's lambs? First, **by being fed himself**. The Lord gave him a breakfast before giving him a commission. You cannot feed lambs, or sheep either, unless you are fed yourself. It is quite right for you to be teaching a great part of the Lord's day, but I think a teacher is very unwise who does not come to hear the Gospel preached and get a meal for his own soul. First be fed, and then feed.

But especially Peter was prepared for feeding the lambs **by being with his Master**. He would never forget that morning, and all the incidents of it. It was Christ's voice that he heard. It was Christ's look that pierced him to the heart. He breathed the air which surrounded the risen Lord. This fellowship with Jesus perfumed Peter's heart and tuned Peter's speech, that he might afterwards go forth and feed the lambs. I commend to you the study of instructive books, but above all I commend the study of Christ. Let Him be your library. Get near to Jesus. An hour's communion with Jesus is the best preparation for teaching either the young or the old.

Peter was also prepared in a more painful way—namely, **by self-examination**. The question came to him three times, *"Simon, son of Jonas, lovest thou Me?...Lovest thou Me?...Lovest thou Me?"* (John 21:15, 16, 17). Often the vessel wants scouring with self-examination before the Lord can fitly use it to convey the living water to thirsting ones. It never hurts a true-hearted man to search his own spirit, and to be searched and tried by his Lord. It is the hypocrite who is afraid of the truth which tests his profession of faith: he dreads trying discourses and trying meditations. But the genuine man wants to know for certain that he really does love Christ. Therefore, he looks within himself and questions and cross-questions himself.

Mainly that self-examination should be exercised concerning our love, because the best preparation for teaching Christ's lambs is love—love for Jesus and for them. We cannot be priests on their behalf unless like Aaron we wear their names upon our breasts. We must love, or we cannot bless. Teaching is poor work when love is gone. It is like a smith working without fire, or a builder without mortar. A shepherd who does not love his sheep is a hireling and not a shepherd: he will flee in the time of danger and leave his flock to the wolf.

Where there is no love, there will be no life. Living lambs are not to be fed by dead men. We preach and teach love. Our subject is the love of God in Christ Jesus. How can we teach this if we have no love ourselves? Our object is to create love in the hearts of those we teach, and to foster it where it already exists. How can we convey the fire if it is not kindled in our own hearts? How can a person promote the flame whose hands are damp and dripping with worldliness and indifference, so that he acts on the child's heart rather as a bucket of water than as a flame of fire?

These lambs of the flock live in the love of Christ. Will they not live in ours? He calls them His lambs, and so they are. Will we not love them for His sake? They were chosen in love and redeemed in love. They have been called in love, washed in love, and fed by love. They will be kept by love until they come to the green pastures on the hilltops of heaven. You and I will be out of gear with the vast machinery of divine love unless our souls are full of affectionate zeal for the good of the beloved ones. Love is the grandest preparation for the ministry, whether exercised in the congregation or in the class. Love, and then feed. If you love, feed. If you do not love, then wait until the Lord has quickened you, and lay not your unhallowed hand to this sacred service.

With the weak of the flock, with the new converts in the flock, with the young children in the flock, **our principal business is to feed**. Every sermon, every lesson, should be a feeding sermon and a feeding lesson. It is of little use to stand and thump the Bible and call out, "Believe, believe, believe!" when nobody knows what is to be believed. I see no use in fiddles and tambourines; neither lambs nor sheep can be fed upon brass bands.

There must be doctrine—solid, sound, gospel doctrine—to constitute real feeding. When you have a roast on the table, then ring the dinner bell; but the bell feeds nobody if no meal is served. Getting children to meet in the morning and the afternoon is a waste of their steps and yours if you do not set before them soul-saving, soul-sustaining truth. Feed the lambs. You need not pipe to them, nor put garlands round their necks, but do feed them.

This feeding is unostentatious, **humble, lowly work**. Do you know the name of a shepherd? I have known the names of one or two who follow that calling, but I never heard anybody speak of them as great men. Their names are not in the papers, nor do we hear of them as a trade with a grievance, claiming to be noticed by the legislature. Shepherds are generally quiet, unobtrusive people. When you look at the shepherd, you would not see any difference between him and the plowman or the carter. He plods on uncomplainingly through the winter. In early spring, he has no rest night or day because the lambs are needing him. This he does year after year, and yet he will never be made a Knight of the Garter, nor even be exalted to the peerage, although he may have done far more useful work than those who are floated into rank upon their own beer barrels.

So is the case of many a faithful teacher of young children. You hear but little about him, yet he is doing grand work for which future ages will call him blessed. His Master knows all about him. We shall hear of him in that day, but perhaps not until then.

Feeding the lambs is **careful work**, too; for lambs cannot be fed on anything you please, especially Christ's lambs. You can soon almost poison young believers with bad teaching. Christ's lambs are all too apt to eat herbs which are deleterious. We need to be cautious where we lead them. If men are to take heed what they hear, how much more should we take heed what we teach? Care must be taken in the work of feeding each lamb separately, and the teaching of each child individually the truth which it is best able to receive.

Moreover, this is **continuous work**. *"Feed My lambs,"* is not for a season, but for all time. Lambs could not live if the shepherd only fed them once a week. I reckon they would die between Sunday and Sunday. Therefore, good teachers of the young look after them throughout the week as they have opportunity, and are careful about their souls with prayer and holy example when they are not teaching them by word of mouth. The shepherdry of lambs is daily, hourly work. When is a shepherd's work over? How many hours a day does he labor? He will tell you that in lambing time, he is never done. He sleeps between times when he can, taking much less than forty winks, and then rousing himself for action. It is so with those who feed Christ's lambs. They rest not until God saves and sanctifies their dear ones.

It is **laborious work**, too. At least, he who does not labor at it will have a terrible account to render. Do you think a minister's life is an easy one? He who makes it so will find it hard enough when he comes to die. Nothing so exhausts a man who is called to it as the care of souls. So it is in measure with all who teach: they cannot do good without spending themselves. You must study the lesson. You must bring forth something fresh to your class. You must instruct and impress. I have no doubt that you are often driven very hard for subject matter and wonder how you will get through the next Sunday. I know you are sorely pressed at times if you are worth your salt. You dare not rush to your class unprepared and offer to the Lord that which costs you nothing. There must be labor if the food is to be wisely placed before the lambs, so that they can receive it.

And all this has to be done in a **singularly choice spirit**. The true shepherd spirit is an amalgam of many precious graces. He is hot with zeal, but he is not fiery with passion. He is gentle, and yet he rules his class. He is loving, but he does not wink at sin. He has power over the lambs, but he is not domineering or sharp. He has cheerfulness, but not levity; freedom, but not license; solemnity, but not gloom. He who cares for lambs should be a lamb himself. Blessed be God, there is a Lamb before the throne who cares for all of us, and does so all the more effectually because He is in all things made like us.

The shepherd spirit is a rare and priceless gift. A successful pastor or a successful teacher in a school will be found to have special characteristics which distinguish him from his fellows. A bird when it is sitting on its eggs, or when the little ones are newly-hatched, has about it a mother spirit, so that it devotes all its life to the feeding of its little ones. Other birds may be taking their pleasure on the wing, but this bird sits still the whole day and night, or else its only flights are to provide for gaping mouths which seem to be never filled. A passion has taken possession of the bird.

Something like this comes over the true soul winner. He would gladly die to win souls. He pines, he pleads, he plods to bless those on whom his heart is set. If these lambs could but be saved, he would pawn half his heaven for it. Sometimes in moments of enthusiasm, he is ready to barter heaven altogether to win souls. Like Paul, he could wish himself accursed, so that they were but saved. This blessed extravagance many cannot understand, because they never felt it. May the Spirit work it in us, so we will act as true shepherds towards the lambs. This is the work: *"Feed My lambs."*

Chapter 5

Of Such Is the Kingdom of Heaven

*But Jesus said, Suffer little children,
and forbid them not, to come unto me: for of
such is the kingdom of heaven.
—Matthew 19:14*

O ur Lord tells the disciples that the Gospel
sets up a kingdom. Was there ever a
kingdom which had no children in it? How,
then, could it grow? Jesus tells us that children
are admitted into the kingdom; not only that
some few are here and there admitted into it,
but, *"of such is the kingdom of God"* (Luke
18:16). I am not inclined to get away from the
plain sense of that expression, nor to suggest
that He merely means that the kingdom con-
sists of those who are like children. It is clear
that He meant such children as those who
were before him—babes and young children—
"of such is the kingdom of God."

There are children in all kingdoms, and there are children in Christ's kingdom. I am not certain that John Newton was not right when he said that the majority of persons who are now in the kingdom of God are children. When I think of all the multitudes of babes that have died, who are now swarming in the streets of heaven, it does seem to me to be a blessed thought that although generation after generation of adults have passed away in unbelief and rebellion, yet enormous multitudes of children have gone streaming up to heaven, saved by the grace of God, through the death of Christ, to sing the high praises of the Lord forever before the eternal throne. *"Of such is the kingdom of heaven."* They give tone and character to the kingdom; it is rather a kingdom of children than of men.

Our Lord tells us that the way of entering the kingdom is by receiving. *"Whosoever shall not receive the kingdom of God as a little child shall in no wise enter therein"* (Luke 18:17). We do not enter into the kingdom of God by working out some deep problem and arriving at its solution; not by fetching something out of ourselves, but by receiving a secret something into us. We come into the kingdom by the kingdom's coming into us: it receives us by our receiving it.

Now, if this entrance into the kingdom depended upon something to be fetched out of

43

the human mind by study and deep thought, then very few children could ever enter it. But it depends upon something to be received, and therefore children may enter. Those children who are of years sufficient to sin, and to be saved by faith, have to listen to the Gospel and to receive it by faith. And they can do this, God the Holy Spirit helping them. There is no doubt about it, because great numbers have done it. I will not say at what age children are first capable of receiving the knowledge of Christ, but it is much earlier than some fancy. We have seen and known children who have given abundant evidence that they have received Christ and have believed in Him at a very early age. Some of them have died triumphantly, and others of them have lived graciously. Some are in our midst, grown men and women now, who are honorable members of the church.

We know that infants enter the kingdom, for we are convinced that all of our race who die in infancy are included in the election of grace, and partake in the redemption worked by our Lord Jesus. Whatever some may think, the whole spirit and tone of the Word of God, as well as the nature of God Himself, lead us to believe that all who die as babes are saved.

How do infants receive the kingdom, for in the same way must we receive it? Certainly children do not receive it by birth or blood, for we are expressly told in John's gospel that the children of God are *"born, not of blood, nor of the will of the flesh, nor of the will of man, but of God"* (John 1:13). All privilege of descent is now abolished, and no babe enters into heaven because it was born of a pious father or mother, neither will any be shut out because his progenitors were atheists or idolaters. My solemn persuasion is that the child of an Islamic, or a Papist, or a Buddhist, or a cannibal, dying in infancy, is as surely saved as the child of the Christian. Salvation by blood or birth there can be none, for the gospel dispensation does not admit of it: if saved, as we assuredly believe they are, infants must be saved simply according to the will and good pleasure of God, because He has made them to be His own.

Children dying in infancy in China and Japan are as truly saved as those dying in England or Scotland. Babes of swarthy mothers, infants born in the kraal of the Hottentot or the wigwam of the Indian are alike saved, and therefore not saved by any outward rite, or by the mystic power of a priesthood. They are raised to the kingdom of heaven by the free and sovereign grace of God.

How are they saved, then? By works? No, for they have never done any. By their natural innocence? No, for if that innocence could have admitted them to heaven, it must also have sufficed to save them from pain and death. If sin is not on them in some form, how is it that they suffer? The imputed sin which makes them die prevents our believing that they claim heaven by right of innocence. They die because of Adam's fall, the sad consequences of their being born of fallen parents. Mark their appealing looks as the dear little ones look up in their sufferings, as if they ask why they must endure so much pain. We look at them with deeper grief because we cannot help them and are made to reflect on the mysterious union of the race in its fall and sorrow. The anguish of the dying little one is proof of Adam's fall, and of its participation in the result.

The dear babes live again, however, because Jesus died and rose again, and they are in Him. They perish, as far as this life is concerned, for a sin which they did not commit. But they also live eternally through a righteousness in which they had no hand, even the righteousness of Jesus Christ, who has redeemed them. We know little of the matter, but we suppose them to undergo regeneration before they enter heaven: for that which is born of the flesh is flesh, and to enter the spiritual world they must be born of the Spirit. But whatever is worked in them, it is clear that they do not enter the kingdom by the force of intellect, or will, or merit, but as a matter of free grace, having no reference to anything that they have done or have felt.

In that same manner you must pass into the kingdom entirely through free grace, and not at all by any power or merit of your own. You will enter heaven as fully by grace as if you had never lived a godly life, nor had practiced a single virtue.

Now we have to think of another sort of children, those who outlive the time of infancy and become children capable of actual sin, and of knowing Christ, and being converted. Many of them enter the kingdom by faith. Now, as these children receive the kingdom of heaven, so must we receive it.

How do the children receive it? I answer, **a child receives the Gospel with humility, with simple faith, and with unworldliness**. Children are not held up to us as an example in all things, for they have faults which we ought to avoid, but they are here praised in this point—the way in which they receive the kingdom. How does a child receive it? First, with humility. He is humble enough to be without prejudice. Take a little child and tell him about Christ Jesus the Savior, and if God blesses the telling of the story of the cross, and he believes it, he receives it without having any wrong views and notions to battle with.

Many a man hears the Gospel with the idea that Christ is merely human. He cannot get rid of that prejudice from his mind, and therefore he does not receive Christ Jesus the

Lord. Another comes to hear the word with the recollection of all that he has heard and read of infidelity, heresy, and profanity. How can he profit until this is removed? Another comes with his mind stuffed with self-righteousness, with a belief in priest craft, or with a reliance upon some form or ceremony. If we could get this lumber out of the soul, there would be some hope; but all this is a hindrance.

Now, the dear child, as he listens to the story of the love of God in Christ Jesus, has none of these prejudices to spoil his hearing. Very likely he does not even know that such evils have been invented by man, and he is blessed in his ignorance. He will find out the evil soon enough; but for the present, he humbly drinks in the Word and prays:

> "Gentle Jesus, meek and mild,
>   Look on me, a little child!
> Pity my simplicity;
>   Suffer me to come to Thee."

Deliverance from preconceived notions is what we greatly need. Just as your little boy or your little girl must believe, even so must you. There is only one way for the shepherd and the sage, the philosopher and the peasant. The little child receives Christ humbly, for he never dreams of merit or purchase. I do not recollect ever having met with a child who had to battle with self-righteousness in coming to Christ.

Chapter 6

As a Little Child

Verily I say unto you, Whosoever shall not receive the kingdom of God as a little child shall in no wise enter therein.
—Luke 18:17

When our Lord blessed the little children He was making His last journey to Jerusalem. It was thus a farewell blessing which He gave to the little ones, and it reminds us of the fact that among His parting words to His disciples, before He was taken up, we find the tender charge, *"Feed My lambs."* The ruling passion was strong upon the great Shepherd of Israel, who *"shall gather the lambs with His arm, and carry them in His bosom"* (Isaiah 40:11). It was fitting that, while He was making His farewell journey, He should bestow His gracious benediction upon the children.

Our Lord Jesus Christ is not among us in person, but we know where He is and that He is clothed with all power in heaven and in earth with which to bless His people. Let us then draw near to Him. Let us seek His touch in the form of fellowship and ask the aid of His intercession. Let us include others in our prayers. Among these let us give our children, and, indeed, all children, a leading place. We know more of Jesus than the women of Palestine did. Let us, therefore, be even more eager than they were to bring our children to Him that He may bless them, and that they may be accepted in Him, even as we ourselves are. Jesus waits to bless. He is not changed in character or impoverished in grace. As He still receives sinners, so does He still bless children. Let none of us be content, whether we are parents or teachers, until He has received our children and has so blessed them that we are sure they have entered the kingdom of God.

When He saw that His disciples were not only hesitant to admit the children to Him, but even rebuked those who brought them, our Savior was much displeased, and called them to Him that He might teach them better. He informed them that, instead of the children being regarded as intruders, they were most welcome by Him. Instead of being interlopers, they had full right of access, for His kingdom is composed of children and childlike persons.

Moreover, He declared that none could enter that kingdom except in the same manner as children enter. He spoke with divine certainty, using His own expressive *"verily,"* and He spoke with the weight of His own personal authority, *"I say unto you."* These prefatory expressions are intended to secure our reverent attention to the fact that so far from the admission of children into the kingdom being unusual or strange, none can find entrance there except that they receive the Gospel as a little child receives it.

It is pretty clear that the disciples thought the children were too insignificant for the Lord's time to be taken up by them. If it had been a prince who wished to come to Jesus, no doubt Peter and the rest of them would have diligently secured him an introduction. But, you see, these were only poor women, with babies, boys, and girls. If it had been an ordinary person, like themselves, they would not have repelled him with rebukes. But mere children? Nursing infants and little children? It was too awful for these to be thrust upon the great Teacher. A word is used about the youthful applicants which may signify children of any age, from infants up to twelve years: surely Jesus had worry enough without the intrusion of these juveniles. He had higher subjects for thought and graver objects of care.

The children were so very little, they were quite beneath His notice: at least, so the disciples thought in their hearts. But if it comes to a matter of insignificance, who can hope to win the divine attention? If we think that children must be little in His sight, what are we? He takes up the isles as a very little thing; the inhabitants of the earth are as grasshoppers. Yes, we are all as nothing. If we were humble we should exclaim, *"Lord, what is man, that Thou art mindful of him? and the son of man, that Thou visitest him?"* (Psalm 8:4). If we dream that the Lord will not notice the little and insignificant, what think we of such a text as this: *"Are not two sparrows sold for a farthing? and one of them shall not fall on the ground without your Father...Fear ye not therefore, ye are of more value than many sparrows"* (Matthew 10:29, 31). Do you imagine that God could care for sparrows, but not care for little children?

The idea of insignificance must be set aside at once. *"Though the Lord be high, yet hath He respect unto the lowly"* (Psalm 138:6). But are little children so insignificant? Do they not populate heaven? Is it not your conviction? It is mine that children make up a very considerable part of the population of the skies. Multitudes of infant feet are treading the streets of the New Jerusalem. Snatched from the breast before they had committed actual sin, delivered from the toilsome pilgrimage of life, they always behold the face of our Father which is in heaven. *"Of such is the kingdom of God."*

Call you these insignificant? Children, who are the most numerous company in the army of the elect, dare you despise them? I might turn the tables and call the adults insignificant, among whom there can be found no more than a small remnant who serve the Lord.

Besides, many children are graciously kept to grow up to man's estate, and therefore we must not think a child insignificant. The child is the father of the man. In him are great possibilities and capacities. His manhood is as yet undeveloped, but it is there. He that trifles with it mars the man. He who tempts the mind of a boy may destroy the soul of a man. A little error injected into the ear of a youth may become deadly in the man when the slow poison at last shall have touched a vital part. Weeds sown in the furrows of childhood will grow with the young man's growth, ripen in his prime, and only decay into a sad corruption when he himself declines.

On the other hand, a truth dropped into a child's heart will also grow and ripen, and his manhood shall see the fruit of it. That child listening in the class to his teacher's gentle voice may develop into a Luther and shake the world with his vehement proclamation of the truth. Who among us can tell? At any rate, with the truth in his heart, the boy will grow up to honor and fear the Lord. Thus will he help keep alive a godly seed in these evil days.

Therefore, let no man despise the young, or think them insignificant. I claim a front place for them. I ask that, if others are kept back, at any rate their feebleness may make room for the little ones. They are the world's future. The past has been, and we cannot alter it. Even the present is gone while we gaze on it. But our hope lies in the future. Therefore, leave room for the children, room for the boys and girls!

I suppose that these grown-up apostles thought that the children's minds were too trifling. They are at their play and their childish mirth. They will regard it only as a pastime to be folded in Jesus' arms. It will be mirth to them, and they will have no idea of the solemnity of their position. Trifling, is it? Children are said to be guilty of trifling! Are you not also triflers? If it comes to an examination on the matter of trifling, who are the greatest triflers, children or full-grown men and women? What is greater trifling than for a man to live for the enjoyment of sensual pleasures, or for a woman to live to dress herself and waste her time in gossiping? More, what is the accumulation of wealth for the sake of it but miserable trifling? Child's play without the amusement! Most men are triflers on a larger scale than children, which is the main difference.

When they trifle, children play with little things. Their toys are so breakable, are they not made on purpose to be trifled with and broken? The child with his trifles is but doing as he should. Alas, I know men and women who trifle with their souls, and with heaven and hell, and eternity. They trifle with God's Word, trifle with God's Son, trifle with God Himself! Charge not children with being frivolous, for their little games often have as much of earnestness about them, and are as useful, as the pursuits of men. Half the councils of our senators and the debates of our parliaments are worse than child's play. The game of war is a far greater folly than the most frolicsome of boyish tricks. Big children are worse triflers than the little ones can ever be. Despise not children for trifling when the whole world is given to folly.

"Yes," say some, "but if we should let the children come to Christ, and if He should bless them, they will soon forget it. No matter how loving His look and how spiritual His words, they will go back to their play and their weak memories will preserve no trace of it at all." This objection we meet in the same manner as the others. Do not grown men forget? What a forgetful generation most preachers address! Truly this is a generation like to that of which Isaiah said, *"Precept must be upon precept, precept upon precept; line upon line, line upon line; here a little, and there a little"* (Isaiah 28:10). Alas, many must have the Gospel preached to them again, and again, and again, until the preacher is nearly weary with his hopeless task; for they are like to men who see their natural faces in a mirror and go their way to forget what manner of men they are. They live in sin still. The Word has no abiding place in their hearts. Forgetfulness! Charge not children with it, lest the accusation be proven against yourselves.

But do the little ones forget? I suppose the events which we best remember in advanced age are the things which happened to us in our earliest days. At any rate, I have shaken hands with grey-headed men who have forgotten nearly all the events which have intervened between their old age and the time of their childhood, but little matters which transpired at home, hymns learned at their mother's knee, and words spoken by their father or sister have lingered with them.

The voices of childhood echo throughout life. The first learned is generally the last forgotten. The young children who heard our Lord's blessing would not forget it. They would have His countenance photographed upon their hearts and never forget His kind and tender smile. Peter, James, John, and the rest of you are all mistaken, and therefore you must suffer the children to come to Jesus.

Perhaps, too, they thought that children had not sufficient capacity. Jesus Christ said such wonderful things that the children could not be supposed to have the capacity to receive them. Yet, indeed, this is a great error, for children readily enter into our Lord's teaching. They never learn to read so quickly from any book as from the New Testament. The words of Jesus are so childlike and so fitted for children that they drink them in better than the words of any other man, however simple he may try to be. Children readily understand the child Jesus.

What is this matter of capacity? What capacity is lacking? The capacity to believe? I tell you, children have more of that than grown-up persons. I am not now speaking of the spiritual part of faith, but as far as the mental faculty is concerned, there is any quantity of the capacity for faith in the heart of a child. His believing faculty has not yet been overloaded by superstition, or perverted by falsehood, or maimed by wicked unbelief. Only let the Holy Spirit consecrate the faculty, and there is enough of it for the production of abundant faith in God.

In what respect are children deficient of capacity? Do they lack capacity for repentance? Assuredly not! Have I not seen a girl weep herself ill because she has done wrong? A tender conscience in many a little boy has made him unutterably miserable when he has been conscious of a fault. Do not some of us recollect the keen arrows of conviction which rankled in our hearts when we were yet children? I distinctly recollect the time when I could not rest because of sin and sought the Lord, while yet a child, with bitter anguish. Children are capable enough of repentance, God the Holy Spirit working it in them. This is no conjecture, for we ourselves are living witnesses.

What, then, do children want in the matter of capacity? "Why, they have not sufficient understanding," says one. Understanding of what? If the religion of Jesus were that of modern thought, if it were such sublime nonsense that none but the so-called cultured class could make heads or tails of it, then children might be incapable of its comprehension. But if indeed it is the Gospel of the poor man's Bible, then there are shallows in it where the tiniest lamb in Jesus' fold may wade without fear of being carried off its feet. It is true that in the Scriptures there are great mysteries, where your leviathans may dive and find no bottom. But the knowledge of these deep things is not essential to salvation, or else few of us would be saved. The things that are essential to salvation are so exceedingly simple that no child need sit down in despair of understanding the things which make for his peace. Christ crucified is not a riddle for sages, but a plain truth for plain people. True, it is meat for men, but it is also milk for babes.

Did you say that children could not love? That, after all, is one of the grandest parts of the education of a Christian. Did you dream that children could not attain to it? No, you did not say that, nor dared you think it, for the capacity for love is great in a child. I would pray that it were always as great in ourselves!

To put the thoughts of the apostles into one or two words: they thought that the children must not come to Christ because they were not like themselves—not men and women. A child is not big enough, tall enough, grown enough, great enough to be blessed by Jesus! So they half-thought. The child must not come to the Master because he is not like the man. How the blessed Savior turns the tables and says, "Say not, the child may not come until he is like a man, but know that you cannot come until you are like him. It is no difficulty in the child that he is not like you. The difficulty is with you, that you are not like the child." Instead of the child needing to wait until he grows up and becomes a man, it is the man who must grow down and become like a child.

"Whoever shall not receive the kingdom of God as a little child, shall in no wise enter therein." Our Lord's words are a complete and all-sufficient answer to the thoughts of His disciples. We may each one, as we read them, learn wisdom. Let us not say, "Would to God

my child were grown like myself that he might come to Christ!" Rather, may we almost wish that we were little children again, could forget much that now we know, could be washed clean from habit and prejudice, and could begin again with a child's freshness, simplicity, and eagerness. As we pray for spiritual childhood, Scripture sets its seal upon the prayer, for it is written, *"Except a man be born again he cannot see the kingdom of God"* (John 3:3); and again, *"Except ye be converted, and become as little children, ye shall not enter into the kingdom of heaven"* (Matthew 18:3).

Now, I wonder whether any have such a thought as the disciples' lingering in brain or heart? I wonder whether you ever think in this fashion? I would not be surprised if you do. I hope it is not quite so common as it used to be, but I used to see in certain quarters among old folks a deep suspicion of youthful piety. The seniors shook their heads at the idea of receiving children into the church. Some ventured to speak of converts as "only a lot of girls and boys," as if they were worse for that. Many, if they hear of a child convert, are very dubious, unless he dies early. Then they believe all about him. If the child lives, they sharpen their axes to have a cut at him by way of examination. He must know all the doctrines, certainly, and he must be supernaturally grave. It is not every grown-up person who knows the higher doctrines of the Word, but if the young person should not know them he is set aside.

Some people expect almost infinite wisdom in a child before they can believe him to be the subject of divine grace. This is monstrous. Then, again, if a believing child should act like a child, some of the fathers of the last generation judged that he could not be converted, as if conversion to Christ added twenty years to our age. Of course, the young convert must not play any more, nor talk in his own childish fashion, or the seniors would be shocked. It was a sort of understood thing that as soon as a child was converted, he was to turn into an old man!

I never could see anything in Scripture to support this theory. However, Scripture was not so much cared for as the judgment of the deeply experienced people, along with the general opinion that it was well to summer and winter all converts before admitting them into the sacred enclosures of the church. Now, if any of you still have an idea in your head hostile to the conversion of children, try to get rid of it, for it is as wrong as wrong can be. If there were two inquirers before me now, a child and a man, and I received from each the same testimony, I should have no more right to distrust the child than to suspect the man. In fact, if suspicion must come in anywhere, it ought rather to be exercised towards the adult than in reference to the child, who is far less likely to be guilty of hypocrisy than the man, and far less likely to have borrowed his words and phrases. Anyway, learn from the Master's words that you are not to try to make the child like yourself, but you are to be transformed until you yourself are like the child.

Chapter 7

"Feed My Lambs"

So when they had dined, Jesus saith to Simon Peter, Simon, son of Jonas, lovest thou me more than these? He saith unto him, Yea, Lord; thou knowest that I love thee. He saith unto him, Feed my lambs.
—John 21:15

The motive for feeding the lambs was to be his Master's self, and not his own self. Had Peter been the first pope of Rome, and had he been like his successors (which indeed he never was), surely it would have been fitting for the Lord to have said to him, "Feed *your* sheep. I commit them to you, O Peter, Vicar of Christ on earth." No, no, no. Peter is to feed them, but they are not his, they are still Christ's. The work that you have to do for Jesus, brothers and sisters, is in no sense for yourselves. Your classes are not your children, but Christ's.

The exhortation which Paul gave was, *"Feed the church of God"* (Acts 20:28). Peter himself wrote in his epistle, *"Feed the flock of God which is among you, taking the oversight thereof, not by constraint, but willingly; not for filthy lucre, but of a ready mind"* (1 Peter 5:2). Let these lambs turn out what they may, the glory is to be to the Master and not to the servant. The whole time spent, labor given, and energy put forth is, every particle, of it to overflow with the praise of Him whose lambs these are.

Yet while this is a self-denying occupation, it is sweetly honorable, too. We may attend to it feeling that it is one of the noblest forms of service. Jesus says, *"My lambs...My sheep"* (John 21:15, 16, 17). Think of them, and wonder that Jesus should commit them to us.

Poor Peter! Surely when that breakfast began, he felt awkward. I put myself into his place, and I know I should hardly have liked to look across the table at Jesus, as I remembered that I denied Him with oaths and curses. Our Lord desired to set Peter quite at his ease by leading him to speak about his love, which had been so seriously placed in question. Like a good doctor he puts in the lancet where the anxiety was festering. He inquires, *"Lovest thou Me?"* It was not because Jesus did not know Peter's love, but so that Peter might know for sure and make a new confession, saying, *"Yea, Lord; Thou knowest that I love Thee."*

The Lord is about to hold a tender controversy with the erring one for a few minutes, that there might never be a controversy between Him and Peter any more. When Peter said, *"Yea, Lord; Thou knowest that I love Thee,"* you may have half thought that the Lord would answer, "Ah, Peter, and I love you." He did not say so, but in a way He did say so.

Perhaps Peter did not see His meaning, but we can because our minds are not confused as Peter's was on that memorable morning. Jesus did in effect say, "I love you so that I trust you with that which I purchased with My heart's blood. The dearest thing I have in all the world is My flock. Simon, I have such confidence in you, I so wholly rely on your integrity as being a sincere lover of Me, that I make you a shepherd to My sheep. These are all I have on earth. I gave everything for them, even My life. Now, Simon, son of Jonas, take care of them for Me." Oh, how tenderly Christ spoke to Peter. It was the great heart of Christ saying, "Poor Peter, come right in and share My dearest cares." Jesus so believed Peter's declaration that He did not tell him so in words, but in deeds. Three times He said it, *"Feed My lambs...feed My sheep...feed My sheep,"* to show how much He loved him. When the Lord Jesus loves a man very much, He gives him much to do or much to suffer.

Many of us have been plucked like brands from the burning, for we were *"alienated and enemies* [of God] *by wicked works"* (Colossians 1:21). Now we are in the church among His friends, and our Savior trusts us with His dearest ones. I wonder if when the prodigal son came back and the father received him, whether on market day the father sent his younger son to market to sell the wheat and bring home the money. Most of you would have said, "I am glad the boy has come back. At the same time, I shall send his elder brother to do the business, for he has always stuck by me."

As for myself, the Lord Jesus took me in as a poor, prodigal son, and it was not many weeks before He entrusted me with the Gospel, that greatest of all treasures. This was a grand love token. I know of none to excel it. The commission given to Peter proved how thoroughly the breach was healed, how fully the sin was forgiven, for Jesus took the man who had cursed and sworn in denial of Him and bade him feed His lambs and sheep. Oh, blessed work, not for yourselves, and yet for yourselves! He that serves himself shall lose himself, but he that loses himself really serves himself after the best possible fashion.

The master motive of a good shepherd is love. We are to feed Christ's lambs out of love.

First, as a **proof of love**. *"If ye love Me, keep My commandments"* (John 14:15). Christ is saying, "If you love Me, *'feed My lambs.'"* If you love Christ, then show it. Show it by doing good to others, by laying your life down to help others, that Jesus may have joy of them.

Next, as an **inflowing of love**. *"Feed My lambs."* If you love Christ a little when you begin to do good, you will soon love Him more. Love grows by active exercise. It is like the blacksmith's arm, which increases its strength by wielding the hammer. Love loves until it loves more, and it loves more until it loves still more; and it loves even more until it loves most of all. Then it is not satisfied, but aspires after enlargement of heart that it may copy yet more fully the perfect model of love in Christ Jesus, the Savior.

Besides being an inflowing of love, the feeding of lambs is an **outflow of love**. How often have we told our Lord that we loved Him when we were preaching. I do not doubt you teachers feel more of the pleasure of love to Jesus when you are busy with your classes than when you are by yourselves at home. A person may go home, sit down, and groan out:

> "'Tis a point I long to know,
>   Oft it causes anxious thought,"

and wipe his forehead and rub his eyes, and get into the dumps without end. But if he will rise up and work for Jesus, the point he longs to know will soon be settled, for love will come pouring out of his heart until he can no longer question whether it is there.

So let us abide in this blessed service for Christ that it may be the delight of love, the very ocean in which love shall swim, the sunlight in which it shall bask. **The recreation of a loving soul is working for Jesus Christ**. Among the highest and most delicious forms of this heavenly recreation is the feeding of young Christians, endeavoring to build them up in knowledge and understanding, that they may become strong in the Lord.

Chapter 8

Timothy and His Teachers

*And that from a child thou hast known the holy
scriptures, which are able to make thee wise
unto salvation through faith
which is in Christ Jesus.*
—2 Timothy 3:15

Nowadays, since the world has in it so few
Christian mothers and grandmothers, the
church has thought it wise to supplement
home instruction by teaching held under her
fostering wing. The church takes under her
maternal care those children who have no such
parents. I regard this as a very blessed institution. I am thankful for the many brothers and
sisters who give their Sundays (many of them
a considerable part of their weekday evenings
also) to teaching other people's children, who
somehow grow to be very much their own.
They endeavor to perform the duties of fathers

and mothers, for God's sake, to those children who are neglected by their own parents. Therein they do well.

Let no Christian parents fall into the delusion that the Sunday school is intended to ease them of their personal duties. The first and most natural condition of things is for Christian parents to train up their own children in the nurture and admonition of the Lord. Let holy grandmothers and gracious mothers, with their husbands, see to it that their own boys and girls are well taught in the Word of the Lord.

Where there are no such Christian parents, it is well and wisely done for godly people to intervene. It is a Christ-like work when another undertakes the duty which the person originally responsible for the task has left undone. The Lord Jesus looks with pleasure upon those who feed His lambs and nurse His babes, for it is not His will that any of these little ones should perish. Timothy had the great privilege of being taught by those whose natural duty it is. But where that great privilege cannot be enjoyed, let us all, as God helps us, try to make up to the children the terrible loss which they endure. Come forward, earnest men and women, and sanctify yourselves for this joyful service.

Note the subject of the instruction. *"From a child thou hast known the holy Scriptures."*

Timothy was led to treat the book of God with great reverence. I lay stress upon that word *"holy Scriptures."* One of the first objects of the Sunday school should be to teach the children great reverence for these holy writings, these inspired Scriptures. The Jews esteemed the Old Testament beyond all price. Though unfortunately many of them fell into a superstitious reverence for the letter and lost the spirit of it, yet were they much to be commended for their profound regard of the holy oracles.

Especially is this feeling of reverence needed nowadays. I meet with men who hold strange views, but I do not care one-half so much about their views, nor about the strangeness of them, as I do about a certain something which I detect at the back of this novel thinking. When I discern that, and if I prove their views to be unscriptural, I have nevertheless proved nothing to them because they do not care about Scripture. Then I have found out a principle far more dangerous than mere doctrinal blundering.

This indifference to Scripture is the great curse of the church at this hour. We can be tolerant of divergent opinions, so long as we perceive an honest intent to follow the Statute Book. But if it comes to this, that the Book itself is of small authority to you, then we have no need of further parley. We are in different camps, and the sooner we recognize this, the better for all parties concerned. If we are to have a church of God at all in the land, Scripture must be regarded as holy, and to be held in reverence. This Scripture was given by holy inspiration and is not the result of dim myths and dubious traditions. Neither has it drifted down to us by the survival of the fittest as one of the best of human books. It must be given to our children, and accepted by ourselves, as the infallible revelation of the Most Holy God. Lay much stress upon this. Tell your children that the Word of the Lord is a pure Word, as silver tried in a furnace of earth, purified seven times. Let their esteem for the Book of God be carried to the highest point.

Observe that Timothy was taught, not only to reverence holy things in general, but especially to know the Scriptures. The teaching of his mother and his grandmother was the teaching of holy Scripture. Suppose we get the children together on Sundays, and then amuse them to make the hours pass away pleasantly, or instruct them as we do during the week in the elements of a moral education—what have we done? We have done nothing worthy of the day or of the church of God.

Suppose that we are particularly careful to teach the children the rules and regulations of our own church, but do not take them to the Scriptures. Suppose that we bring before them a book which is set up as the standard of our church, but do not dwell upon the Bible—what have we done? That standard may or may not be correct, and we may, therefore, have taught our children truth or have taught them error. But if we keep to holy Scripture, we cannot go wrong. With such a standard, we know that we are right. This Book is the Word of God, and if we teach it, we teach that which the Lord will accept and bless. O dear teachers—and I speak here to myself also—let our teaching be more and more scriptural!

Fret not if our classes forget what we say, but pray that they remember what the Lord says. May divine truths about sin, righteousness, and the judgment to come be written on their hearts! May revealed truths concerning the love of God, the grace of our Lord Jesus Christ, and the work of the Holy Ghost never be forgotten by them! May they know the virtue and necessity of the atoning blood of our Lord, the power of His resurrection, and the glory of His second coming! May the doctrines of grace be engraved as with a pen of iron upon their minds and written as with the point of a diamond upon their hearts, never to be erased! If we can secure this, we have not lived in vain. The generation now ruling seems bent on departing from the eternal truth of God. But we shall not despair if the Gospel is impressed upon the memory of the rising race.

Once more upon this point: it appears that young Timothy was so taught as a child that the teaching was effective. *"Thou hast known the holy Scriptures,"* says Paul. It is a good deal to say of a child that he has *"known the holy Scriptures."* You may say, "I have taught the children the Scriptures," but that they have known them is quite another thing. Do all of you who are grown up know the Scriptures? I fear that although knowledge in general increases, knowledge of the Scriptures is far too rare. If we were now to hold an examination, I am afraid that some of you would hardly shine in the lists at the end.

But here was a little child who knew the holy Scriptures. This is to say, he had a remarkable acquaintance with them. Children can learn that. It is by no means an impossible attainment. God blessing your efforts, dear friends, your children may know all of Scripture that is necessary to their salvation. They may have as true an idea of sin as their mother has. They may have as clear a view of the atonement as their grandmother can have. They may have as distinct a faith in Jesus as any of us can have. The things that make for our peace require no length of experience to prepare us for receiving them. They are among the simplicities of thought. He may run that reads them, and a child may read them as soon as he can run.

The opinion that children cannot receive the whole truth of the Gospel is a great mistake, for their child's condition is a help rather than a hindrance. Older folk must become as little children before they can enter the kingdom. Do lay a good groundwork for the children. Let not Sunday-school work be slurred, nor done in a slovenly manner. Teach the holy Scriptures. Let the Scriptures be consulted rather than any human book.

This work of instilling the Word was quickened by a saving faith in Timothy. The Scriptures do not save, but they are able to make a man *"wise unto salvation."* Children may know the Scriptures, and yet not be children of God. Faith in Jesus Christ is that grace which brings immediate salvation. Many dear children are called of God so early that they cannot precisely tell when they were converted, but they were converted. They, at some time or other, have passed from death to life. You could not have told this morning, by observation, the moment when the sun rose, but it did rise. There was a time when it was below the horizon, and another time when it had risen above it. The moment, whether we see it or not, in which a child is really saved, is when he believes in the Lord Jesus Christ.

Perhaps for years Lois and Eunice had been teaching the Old Testament to Timothy, while they themselves did not know the Lord

Jesus. If so, they were teaching him the type without the anti-type, the riddles without the answers. However, it was good teaching, since it was all the truth which they then knew.

How much happier, however, is our task, since we are able to teach concerning the Lord Jesus so plainly, having the New Testament to explain the Old! May we hope that even earlier in life than Timothy, our dear children may catch the thought that Christ Jesus is the sum and substance of holy Scripture, and so by faith in Him may receive power to become the sons of God! I mention this, simple as it is, because I want all teachers to feel that if their children do not as yet know all the doctrines of the Bible, and if there are certain higher or deeper truths which their minds have not yet grasped, still children are saved as soon as they are *wise unto salvation through faith which is in Christ Jesus.* Faith in Jesus, as He is set forth in Scripture, will surely save. *"If thou believest with all thine heart, thou mayest"* (Acts 8:37), said Philip to the eunuch. We say the same to every child, "You may confess your faith if you have faith in Jesus to confess. If you believe that Jesus is the Christ, and so put your trust in Him, you are as truly saved as though gray hairs adorned your brow."

By this faith in Christ Jesus, we continue and advance in salvation. The moment we believe in Christ, we are saved. But we are not at once as wise as we may be, or hope to be. We may be, as it were, saved unintelligently—I mean, of course, comparatively so; but it is desirable that we should be able to give a reason for the hope that is in us (see 1 Peter 3:15), and so be wise unto salvation. By faith children become little disciples, and by faith they go on to become more proficient. How are we to go on to wisdom? Not by quitting the way of faith, but by keeping to that same faith in Christ Jesus by which we began to learn.

In the school of grace, faith is the great faculty by which we make advances in wisdom. If, by faith, you have been able to say A and B and C, it must be by faith that you will go on to say D and E and F, until you come to the end of the alphabet and be an expert in the Book of Wisdom. If, by faith, you can read in the spelling book of simple faith, by the same faith in Christ Jesus you must go on to read in the classics of full assurance and become a scribe well instructed in the things of the kingdom. Therefore, keep close to the practice of faith, from which so many are turning aside.

In these times, men look to make progress by what they call thought, by which they mean vain imagination and speculation. We cannot advance a step by doubt. True progress is only by faith. There are no such things as "stepping stones" in or of our dead selves, unless they are stones to death and destruction. The only stepping stones to life and heaven are to be found in the truth of God revealed to our faith. Believe God, and you have made progress.

So let us constantly pray for our children, that they may know and believe more and more. The Scripture is able to make them *"wise unto salvation,"* but only *"through faith which is in Christ Jesus."* Faith is the result to aim at: faith in the appointed, anointed, and exalted Savior. This is the anchorage to which we would bring these little ships, for here they will abide in perfect safety.

Sound instruction in Scripture, when activated by a living faith, creates a solid character. The man who from a child has known the holy Scriptures, when he obtains faith in Christ, will be grounded and settled on the abiding principles of God's unchanging Word.

O teachers, see what you may do! In your schools sit our future evangelists. In that infant class sits an apostle to some distant land. There may come under your training hand, my sister, a future father in Israel. There will come under your teaching, my brother, those who are to bear the banners of the Lord in the thick of the fray. The ages look to you each time your class assembles. Oh, that God may help you to do your part well! We pray with one heart and one soul that the Lord Jesus Christ may be with our Sunday schools from this day and until He comes.

Chapter 9

"What Mean Ye by This Service?"

*And it shall come to pass, when your children
shall say unto you, What mean ye by this
service? That ye shall say, It is the sacrifice
of the LORD'S passover, who passed over the
houses of the children of Israel in Egypt,
when he smote the Egyptians,
and delivered our houses.*
—Exodus 12:26-27

We should view everything in this world by
the light of redemption, and then we
shall view it correctly. It makes a wonderful
change whether you view Providence from the
standpoint of human merit or from the foot of
the cross. We see nothing truly until Jesus is
our light. Everything is seen in its reality when
you look through the glass, the ruby glass of
the atoning sacrifice. Use this telescope of the
cross, and you will see far and clear: look

through the cross at sinners, saints, and sin. Look at the world's joys and sorrows through the cross, look at heaven and hell through the cross. See how conspicuous the blood of the Passover was meant to be, and then learn from this to make much of the sacrifice of Jesus— yes, to make everything of it, for Christ is all.

We read in Deuteronomy concerning the commandments of the Lord, as follows: *"And thou shalt bind them for a sign upon thine hand, and they shall be as frontlets between thine eyes. And thou shalt write them upon the posts of thy house, and on thy gates"* (Deuteronomy 6:8). See, then, that the law is to be engraved by the memorials of the blood.

In Switzerland, in the Protestant villages, you have seen texts of Scripture upon the doorposts. I half wish we had that custom in England. How much of the Gospel might be preached to wayfarers if texts of Scripture were over Christian people's doors! It might be ridiculed as Pharisaical, but we could get over that. Few are liable to that charge in these days through being overly religious. I like to see texts of Scripture in our houses, in all the rooms, on the cornices, and on the walls. But outside on the door—what a capital advertisement the Gospel might get at a cheap rate!

But note, that when the Jew wrote upon his doorposts a promise, or a precept, or a doctrine, he had to write upon a surface stained with blood. When the next year's Passover came round he had to sprinkle the blood with the hyssop right over the writing. It seems to me so delightful to think of the law of God in connection with that atoning sacrifice, which has magnified it and made it honorable. God's commands come to me as a redeemed man. his promises are to me as a blood-bought man. His teaching instructs me as one for whom atonement has been made. The law in the hand of Christ is not a sword to slay us, but a jewel to enrich us. All truth taken in connection with the cross is greatly enhanced in value. Holy Scripture itself becomes dear to a sevenfold degree when we see that it comes to us as the redeemed of the Lord and bears upon its every page marks of those dear hands which were nailed to the tree for us.

You now see how everything was done that could well be thought of to bring the blood of the Paschal lamb into a high position in the esteem of the people whom the Lord brought out of Egypt. You and I must do everything we can think of to bring forward, and keep before men forever, the precious doctrine of the atoning sacrifice of Christ. He was made sin for us though He knew no sin, that we might be made the righteousness of God in Him.

And now I will remind you of the institution that was connected with the remembrance of the Passover. *"It shall come to pass, when your children shall say unto you, What mean ye by this service? that ye shall say, It is the sacrifice of the Lord's Passover."* Curiosity should be excited in the minds of our children. Oh, that we could get them to ask questions about the things of God! Some of them inquire very early, others of them seem diseased with much the same indifference as older folks. With both orders of mind, we have to deal.

It is well to explain to children the ordinance of the Lord's Supper, for this shows forth the death of Christ in symbol. I regret that children do not see this ordinance more often. Baptism and the Lord's Supper should both be placed in view of the rising generation, that they may then ask us, *"What mean ye by this?"*

Now, the Lord's Supper is a perennial gospel sermon, and it turns mainly upon the sacrifice for sin. You may banish the doctrine of the atonement from the pulpit, but it will always live in the church through the Lord's Supper. You cannot explain that broken bread and that cup filled with the fruit of the vine, without reference to our Lord's atoning death. You cannot explain *"the communion of the body of Christ"* (1 Corinthians 10:16) without bringing in, in some form or other, the death of Jesus in our place and stead. Let your little ones, then, see the Lord's Supper, and let them be told most clearly what it sets forth.

If not the Lord's Supper—for that is not the thing itself, but only the shadow of the glorious fact—dwell much and often in their presence upon the sufferings and death of our Redeemer. Let them think of Gethsemane, Gabbatha, and Golgotha. Let them learn to sing in plaintive tones of Him who laid down His life for us. Tell them who it was that suffered and why. Yes, though the hymn is hardly to my taste in some of its expressions, I would have the children sing:

"There is a green hill far away,
    Without a city wall."

I would have them learn such lines as these:

"He knew how wicked we had been,
    And knew that God must punish sin;
So out of pity Jesus said
    He'd bear the punishment instead."

And when attention is excited about the best of themes, let us be ready to explain the great transaction by which God is just, and yet sinners are justified. Children can well understand the doctrine of the expiatory sacrifice. Iit was meant to be a Gospel for the youngest. The Gospel of substitution is a simplicity, though it is a mystery. We ought not to be content until our little ones know and trust in their finished Sacrifice. This is essential knowledge, and the key to all other spiritual teaching. May our dear children know the cross, and they will have begun well. With all their getting, may they get an understanding of this (see Proverbs 4:7). Then they will have the foundation rightly laid.

This will necessitate your teaching the child his need of a Savior. You must not hold back from this necessary task. Do not flatter the child with delusive rubbish about his nature being good and needing to be developed. Tell him he must be born again. Don't bolster him up with the notion of his own innocence, but show him his sin. Mention the childish sins to which he is prone, and pray the Holy Spirit to work conviction in his heart and conscience. Deal with the young in much the same way as you would with the old. Be thorough and honest with them. Flimsy religion is never good for young or old. These boys and girls need pardon through the precious blood as surely as any of us.

Do not hesitate to tell the child of his ruin, or else he will not desire the remedy. Tell him also of the punishment of sin, and warn him of its terror. Be tender, but be true. Do not hide from the youthful sinner the truth, however terrible it may be. Now that he has come to years of responsibility, if he believes not in Christ, it will go ill with him at the last great day. Set before him the judgment seat, and remind him that he will have to give an account of things done in the body. Labor to arouse the conscience. Pray that God the Holy Spirit would work through you until the heart becomes tender and the mind perceives the need of the great salvation.

Children need to learn the doctrine of the cross that they may find immediate salvation. I thank God that in our Sunday school we believe in the salvation of children as children. It has been my joy to see so very many boys and girls who have come forward to confess their faith in Christ! And I again wish to say that the best converts, the clearest converts, the most intelligent converts we have ever had have been the young ones. Instead of there being any deficiency in their knowledge of the Word of God and the doctrines of grace, we have usually found them to have a very delightful acquaintance with the great cardinal truths of Christ. Many of these dear children have been able to speak of the things of God with great pleasure of heart and force of understanding. Go on, dear teachers, and believe that God will save your children. Be not content to sow principles in their minds which may possibly develop in after years, but be working for immediate conversion.

Expect fruit in your children while they are children. Pray for them that they may not run into the world and fall into the evils of outward sin, and then come back with broken bones to the Good Shepherd. Rather, pray that they may by God's rich grace be kept from the paths of the destroyer and grow up in the fold of Christ, first as lambs of His flock, and then as sheep of His hand.

One thing I am sure of, and that is, that if we teach the children the doctrine of the atonement in the most unmistakable terms, we will be doing ourselves good. I sometimes hope that God will revive His church and restore her to her ancient faith by a gracious work among children. If He would bring into our churches a large influx of young people, how it would tend to quicken the sluggish blood of the supine and sleepy! Child Christians tend to keep the house alive. Oh, for more of them!

If the Lord will help us to teach the children, we will be teaching ourselves. There is no way of learning like teaching, and you do not know a thing until you can teach it to another. You do not thoroughly know any truth until you can put it before a child so that he can see it. In trying to make a little child understand the doctrine of the atonement, you will get clearer views of it yourselves. I, therefore, recommend the holy exercise to you.

What a mercy it will be if our children are thoroughly grounded in the doctrine of redemption by Christ! If they are warned against the false gospels of this evil age, and if they are taught to rest on the eternal rock of Christ's finished work, we may hope to have a generation following us which will maintain the faith and will be better than their fathers. Your Sunday schools are admirable, but what is their purpose if you do not teach the Gospel in them? You get children together and keep them quiet for an hour-and-a-half, and then send them home; but what is the good of it? It may bring some quiet to their fathers and mothers, and that is, perhaps, why they send them to the school; but all the real good lies in what is taught the children.

The most fundamental truth should be made most prominent. And what is this but the cross? Some talk to children about such things as being good boys and girls; that is to say, they preach the law to the children, though they would preach the Gospel to grown-up people. Is this honest? Is this wise? Children need the Gospel, the whole Gospel, the unadulterated Gospel. They ought to have it. If they are taught of the Spirit of God, they are as capable of receiving it as persons of ripe years. Teach the little ones that Jesus died, the just for the unjust, to bring us to God.

Very, very confidently do I leave this work in the hands of teachers. I never knew a nobler body of Christian men and women, for they are as earnest in their attachment to the Gospel as they are eager for the winning of souls. Be encouraged: the God who has saved so many of your children is going to save very many more of them, and we shall have great joy as we see hundreds brought to Christ.

Chapter 10

Samuel and His Teachers

Therefore Eli said unto Samuel, Go, lie down.
and it shall be, if he call thee, that thou shalt
say, Speak, LORD; for thy servant heareth. So
Samuel went and lay down in his place.
—1 Samuel 3:9

In the days of Eli, the word of the Lord was precious, and there was no open vision. It was well when the word did come, that one chosen individual had the hearing ear to receive it and the obedient heart to perform it. Eli failed to tutor his sons to be the willing servants and the attentive hearers of the Lord's word. In this he was without the excuse of inability, since he successfully trained the child Samuel in reverent attention to the divine will. O that those who are diligent about the souls of others, would look well to their own households!

Alas, poor Eli, like many in our day, who must say, *"They made me keeper of the vineyards, but mine own vineyard have I not kept"* (Song of Solomon 1:6). As often as he looked upon the gracious child, Samuel, he must have felt the heartache. When he remembered his own neglected and unchastened sons, and how they had made themselves vile before all Israel, Samuel was the living witness of what grace can work where children are trained up in God's fear, and Hophni and Phineas were sad specimens of what parental indulgence will produce in the children of the best of men. Ah, Eli, if you had been as careful with your own sons as with the son of Hannah, they would not have been such men of Belial, nor would Israel have abhorred the offering of the Lord because of the fornication which those priestly reprobates committed at the very door of the tabernacle. O for grace to nurse our little ones for the Lord, that they may hear the Lord when He is pleased to speak to them!

Samuel was blessed with a gracious father, and what is of even more importance, he was the child of an eminently holy mother. Hannah was a woman of great poetic talent, as appears from her memorable song: *"My heart rejoiceth in the Lord, mine horn is exalted in the Lord; my mouth is enlarged over mine enemies, because I rejoiced in Thy salvation"* (1 Samuel 2:1). The soul of poetry lives in every line. A brave but chastened spirit breathes in every sentence. Even Mary, the most blessed among women, could do no other than use expressions of similar importance.

Better still, Hannah was a woman of great prayer. She had been a woman of a sorrowful spirit, but her prayers at last returned to her in blessing, and she had this son given her of the Lord. He was very dear to his mother's heart. She, therefore, to show her gratitude, and in fulfillment of the vow which in her anguish she had vowed unto the Lord, would consecrate the best thing she had; she presented her son before the Lord in Shiloh. This should be a lesson to all godly parents, to see to it that they dedicate their children unto God.

How highly favored will we be if our children are all like Isaac—children of the promise! What blessed parents would we be if we saw our children all rise up to call the Redeemer *"blessed"*! It has been the great blessing of some of you to see all your children numbered with the people of God: all your jewels are now in Jehovah's casket. In their early childhood, you gave them to God and dedicated them to Him in earnest prayer. Now the Lord has given you your petition which you asked of Him. I like our friends to hold services in their houses when their family increases. It seems good and profitable for friends to assemble, and prayer to be offered that the child may be an inheritor of the promises, that he may be called early by mighty grace, and that he may be received into the divine family.

You will perceive that, as Samuel was put under Eli's care and tutelage, Eli instructed him in some degree in the spirit of religion. However, he does not appear to have explained to him the peculiar form and nature of those special and particular manifestations of God which were given to His prophets. Eli little dreamed, I dare say, that Samuel would ever be himself the subject of them. On that memorable night, when towards morning the lamp of God was about to go out, the Lord cried, *"Samuel, Samuel"* (1 Samuel 3:10). The young child was not able to discern—for he had not been taught—that it was the voice of God and not the voice of man.

That Samuel had learned the spirit of true religion, is indicated by his instantaneous obedience, and the habit of obedience became a valuable guide to him in the perplexities of that eventful hour. He ran to Eli and said, *"Here am I, for thou didst call me"* (1 Samuel 3:6). Though this is repeated three times, yet the child seemed not to loath leaving his warm bed and running to his foster father to see if he could get him any comfort that his old age might require during the night, or otherwise do his bidding. This is a sure sign that the child had acquired the healthy principle of obedience, though he did not understand the mystery of the prophetic call. Better far to have the young heart trained to bear the yoke than to fill the childish head with knowledge, however valuable. An ounce of obedience is better than a ton of learning.

When Eli perceived that God had called the child, he taught him his first little prayer. It is a very short one, but it is a very full one— *"Speak, LORD; for Thy servant heareth"* (1 Samuel 3:9). Let the Christian parent explain to the child what prayer is. Tell him that God answers prayer. Direct him to the Savior. Then urge him to express his desires in his own language, both when he rises, and when he goes to rest. Gather the little ones around your knee and listen to their words, suggesting to them their needs and reminding them of God's gracious promises.

You will be amazed, and, I may add, sometimes amused, too. But you will be frequently surprised at the expressions they will use, the confessions they will make, the desires they will utter. I am certain that any Christian person, standing within ear-shot and listening to the simple prayer of a little child earnestly asking God for what it thinks it wants, would never afterwards wish to teach a child a form. Rather, he would admit that, as a matter of education of the heart, the extemporaneous utterance was infinitely superior to the best form, and that the form should be given up forever.

However, do not let me speak too sweepingly. If you must teach your child to say a form of prayer, at least take care that you do not teach him to say anything which is not true. If you teach your children a catechism, mind that it is thoroughly scriptural, or you may train them up to tell falsehoods. Teach him nothing but the truth as it is in Jesus, so far as he can learn it, and pray the Holy Spirit to write that truth upon his heart. Better to supply no signposts to the young traveler than to mislead him with false ones. The light of a wrecker's beacon is worse than darkness.

Teach our youth to make untruthful statements in religious matters, and atheism can scarcely do more to corrupt their minds. Formal religion is a deadly foe to vital godliness. If you teach a catechism, or if you teach a form of prayer to your little ones, let it be all true. As far as possible, never put into a child's mouth a word which the child cannot truly say from his heart.

We must be more careful about truthfulness and correctness in speech. If a child looked out of a window at anything going on in the street, and then told you that he saw it from the door, you ought to make him tell the tale over again, so as to impress upon him the necessity of being truthful in every respect.

Especially in things connected with religion, keep your child back from any form until he has a right to be a partaker of it. Never encourage him to come to the Lord's Table unless you really believe that there is a work of grace in his heart. Why would you lead him to eat and drink to his own damnation?

Insist with all your heart that religion is a solemn reality not to be mimicked or pretended. Seek to bring the child to understand that there is no vice more abhorrent before God than hypocrisy. Do not make your young Samuel a young hypocrite, but train up your darling to speak before the Lord with a deep solemnity and a conscientious truthfulness. Let him never dare to say, either in answer to a catechismal question, or as a form of prayer, anything which is not positively true. If you must have a form of prayer, let it not express such desires as a child never had, but let it be adapted to his young capacity.

It is said of the Reverend John James:

"Like most men who have been eminent and honored in the Church of Christ, he had a godly mother, who was wont to take her children to her chamber, and with each separately to pray for the salvation of their souls. This exercise, which fulfilled her own responsibility, was molding the character of her children, and most, if not all of them, rose up to call her blessed. When did such means ever fail?"

I beseech you, Sunday-school teachers—though I scarcely need to do so, for I know how zealous you are in this matter—as soon as you see the first peep of day in your children, encourage their young desires. Believe in the conversion of children, while they are children. Believe that the Lord can call them by His grace, can renew their hearts, can give them a part and a lot among His people long before they reach the prime of life.

Chapter 11

Instructions for Teachers and Parents

*Come, ye children, hearken unto me; I will
teach you the fear of the LORD.*
—*Psalm 34:11*

First, get the children to come to your
school. The great complaint with some
teachers is that they cannot obtain scholars. In
London, we are having a canvass of the children, which is a good idea to implement. You
ought to have a canvass of every country village and every market town, and get into the
Sunday school every child you can. My advice
to you is, get the children to come by all fair
and right means.

Do not bribe them. That is a plan to which
we strongly object. It is only adopted in schools
of the lowest order, schools of so mean a class
that even the fathers and mothers of the children have too much sense to send them there.

"But, then, Farmer Brown won't employ them; or the squire will turn them out of their situations; or, if the children don't go to the school on Sundays, they won't be allowed on weekdays." Oh, that beggarly trick of bribing! I wish there were an end to it. It only shows the weakness, degradation, and abomination of a sect that cannot succeed without using so mean a system.

But with the exception of that method, do not be very particular how you get the children to school. Why, if I could not get people to come to my chapel by preaching in a black coat, I would have regimentals tomorrow. I would have a congregation somehow. Better do strange things than have an empty chapel, or an empty schoolroom.

When I was in Scotland, we sent a bellman around in a village to secure an audience, and the plan was eminently successful. Spare no right means, but do get the children in. I have known ministers who have gone out into the streets on Sunday afternoon, talked to the children who were playing about, and so induced them to come to the school. This is what an earnest teacher will do. He will say, "John, come into our school. You cannot imagine what a nice place it is." Then he gets the children to come. In his kind, winning manner, he tells them stories and anecdotes about girls and boys who love the Savior. In this way, the school is filled. Go and catch the children. There is no law against it. All is fair in war against the devil. So my first instruction is, get the children, and get them anyway that you can.

Next, get the children to love you, if you can. *"Come, ye children, hearken unto me."* You know how we used to be taught in the dame's school, how we stood up with our hands behind us to repeat our lessons. That was not David's plan. "Come, children, come here and sit on my knee." "Oh!" thinks the child, "how nice to have such a teacher, a teacher who will let me come near him, a teacher who does not say, 'Go,' but 'Come!'" The fault of many teachers is that they do not get their children near them, but endeavor to foster in their scholars a kind of awful respect.

Before you can teach children, you must get the silver key of kindness to unlock their hearts, and so secure their attention. Say, *"Come, ye children."* We have known some good men who were objects of abhorrence to children. You remember the story of two little boys who were one day asked if they would like to go to heaven; they, much to their teacher's astonishment, said that they really would not. When they were asked, "Why not?" one of them said, "I would not like to go to heaven because grandpa would be there, and he would be sure to say, 'Get along, boys; be off with you!' I should not like to be in heaven with grandpa." So, if a boy has a teacher who talks to him about Jesus, but who always wears a sour look, what does the boy think? "I wonder whether Jesus is like you; if so, I shouldn't like Him."

Then, there is another teacher, who, if he is provoked ever so little, boxes the child's ears. At the same time, he teaches the child that he should forgive others and be kind to them. "Well," thinks the lad, "that is very pretty, no doubt, but my teacher doesn't show me how to do it." If you drive a boy from you, your power over him is gone, for you will not be able to teach him anything. It is of no avail to attempt teaching those who do not love you. So, try and make them love you, and then they will learn anything from you.

Next, get the children's attention. *"Come, ye children, hearken unto me."* If they are not attentive, you may talk, but you will speak to no purpose whatever. If they do not listen, you go through your labor as an unmeaning drudgery to yourselves and to your scholars, too. You can do nothing without securing their attention. "That is just what I cannot do," says one. Well, that depends on you: if you give them something worth attending to, they will listen. Give them something worth hearing, and they will certainly be all ears. This rule may not be universal, but very nearly so.

Don't forget to give them a few anecdotes. Anecdotes are very much objected to by critics of sermons, who say they ought not to be used in the pulpit. But some of us know better than that. We know what will wake a congregation up. We can testify, from experience, that a few anecdotes here and there are first-rate things to get the attention of people who will not listen to dry doctrine.

Do try to gather as many good illustrations in the week as you possibly can. Wherever you go, if you are really a wise teacher, you can always find something to make into a tale to tell your children. Then, when your scholars get dull, and you are losing their attention, say to them, "Do you know the Five Bells?" If there is such a place in the village, they all open their eyes directly; or you ask, "Do know the turning against the Red Lion?" Then tell them something you have read or heard which will secure their attention to the lesson. A dear child once said, "Father, I like to hear Mr. So-and-So preach, because he puts so many 'likes' into his sermon—'like this, and like that.'" Yes, children always love those "likes."

Make parables, pictures, figures for them, and you will always have their attention. I am sure, if I were a boy listening to some of you, unless you told me a tale now and then, you would see the back of my head as often as my face. If I sat in a hot schoolroom, I do not know but that my head would nod and I would go to sleep. I might be playing with Tom on my left and doing as many strange things as the rest, if you did not strive to interest me. Remember, then, to make your scholars *"hearken."*

Chapter 12

A Model Lesson for Teachers

Keep thy tongue from evil, and thy lips from speaking guile. Depart from evil, and do good; seek peace, and pursue it.
—*Psalm 34:13-14*

Teach your students morality, just as David did. Now, we never teach morality as the way of salvation. God forbid we should ever mix man's works in any way with the redemption which is in Christ Jesus! *"By grace are ye saved through faith, and that not of yourselves, it is the gift of God"* (Ephesians 2:8).

We **teach morality** while we teach spirituality. I have always found that the Gospel produces the best morality in all the world. I would have a Sunday-school teacher watchful over the morals of the boys and girls under his care, speaking to them very particularly of those sins which are most common to youth. He may honestly and conveniently say many things to his children which no one else can say, especially when reminding them of the sin of lying, so common with children, or the sin of petty theft, or of disobedience to parents, or of breaking the Sabbath.

I would have the teacher be very particular in mentioning these evils one by one, for it is of little avail talking to them about sins as a whole. You must take them one by one, just as David did. First look after the tongue: *"Keep thy tongue from evil, and thy lips from speaking guile."* Then look after the whole conduct: *"Depart from evil, and do good; seek peace, and pursue it."* If the child's soul is not saved by other parts of the teaching, this part may have a beneficial effect upon his life, and so far so good.

However, morality by itself is a comparatively small thing. The best part of what you teach is godliness. I did not say *religion*, but **godliness**. Many people are religious after a fashion, without being godly. Many have all the externals of godliness, all the outside signs of piety. Such men we call "religious," but they have no right thought about God. They think about their place of worship, their Sunday, their books, but nothing about God. He who does not respect God, pray to God, and love

God, is an ungodly man, whatever his external religion may be.

Labor to teach the child always to have an eye toward God. Write on his memory these words, *"Thou God seest me"* (Genesis 16:13). Bid him remember that his every act and thought are under the eye of God. No Sunday-school teacher discharges his duty unless he constantly lays stress upon the fact that there is a God who notices everything that happens. Oh, that we were more godly ourselves, that we talked more of godliness, and that we loved godliness better!

The third lesson to be taught is the **evil of sin**. If the child does not learn that lesson, he will never learn the way to heaven. None of us ever knew what a Savior Christ was until we knew what an evil thing sin was. If the Holy Ghost does not teach us the exceeding sinfulness of sin, we will never know the blessedness of salvation. Let us seek His grace, then, when we teach, that we may always be able to lay stress upon the abominable nature of sin. *"The face of the Lord is against them that do evil, to cut off the remembrance of them from the earth"* (Psalm 34:16). Do not spare your child: let him know what sin leads to. Do not, like some people, be afraid of speaking plainly and openly concerning the consequences of sin.

I have heard of a father, one of whose sons, a very ungodly young man, died in a very sudden manner. The father did not, as some would have done, say to his family, "We hope your brother has gone to heaven." Instead, overcoming his natural feelings, he was enabled by divine grace to assemble his other children together and to say to them, "My sons and daughters, your brother is dead. I fear he is in hell. You knew his life and conduct. You saw how he behaved. Now God has snatched him away in his sins." Then he solemnly told them of the place of woe to which he believed —yes, with most certainty knew his son had gone—begging them to shun it and to flee from the wrath to come. Thus, he was the means of bringing his children to serious thought. But had he acted, as some would have done, with tenderness of heart, but not with honesty of purpose, he would have said he hoped his son had gone to heaven. What would the other children have thought about that? "If he is gone to heaven, there is no need for us to fear. We may live as we like." No, no!

It is not unchristian to say of some men that they have gone to hell, when we have seen that their lives have been hellish lives. But it is asked, "Can you judge your fellow creatures?" No, but I can know them by their fruits. I do not judge or condemn them. They judge themselves. I have seen their sins go beforehand to judgment, and I do not doubt that they will follow. "But may they not be saved at the last hour?" I have heard of one person who was, but I do not know if there ever was another, and I can not tell that there ever will be another. Be honest with your children and teach them, by the help of God, that *"evil shall slay the wicked"* (Psalm 34:21).

But you will not have done half enough unless you teach carefully the fourth lesson: the **absolute necessity of a change of heart**. *"The Lord is nigh unto them that are of a broken heart; and saveth such as be of a contrite spirit"* (Psalm 34:18). May God enable us to keep this constantly before the minds of the taught that there must be a broken heart and a contrite spirit; that good works will be of no avail unless there is a new nature; that the most arduous duties and the most earnest prayers will all be nothing, unless there is a true, thorough repentance for sin and an entire forsaking of sin through the grace and mercy of God! Be sure, whatever you leave out, that you teach the children the three *R*'s— Ruin, Redemption, and Regeneration. Tell the children they are ruined by the fall, and that there is salvation for them only by being redeemed by the blood of Jesus Christ and regenerated by the Holy Spirit. Keep constantly before them these vital truths, and then you will have the pleasing task of telling them the sweet subject of the closing lesson.

In the fifth place, tell the children of the **joy and blessedness of being Christians**. *"The Lord redeemeth the soul of His servants: and none of them that trust in Him shall be desolate"* (Psalm 34:22). I need not tell you how to talk about that theme. If you know what it is to be a Christian, you will never be short of subject matter. When we get on this topic, our mind cares not to speak. It would rather revel in its bliss. Truly was it said, *"Blessed is he whose transgression is forgiven, whose sin is covered"* (Psalm 32:1). *"Blessed is that man that maketh the Lord his trust."* (Psalm 40:4). Blessed is the man, the woman, or the child who trusts in Jesus Christ and whose hope is in Him. Always stress this point: that the righteous are a blessed people; that the chosen family of God, redeemed by blood and saved by power, are a blessed people while here below; and that they will be a blessed people forever in heaven.

Let your children see that you belong to that blessed company. If they know you are in trouble, if it is at all possible with you, come to your class with a smiling face. Then your scholars may be able to say, "My teacher is a blessed man, although he is bowed down by his troubles." Always seek to keep a joyous countenance, so that your boys and girls may know that your religion is a blessed reality. Let this be one main point of your teaching: *"Many are*

the afflictions of the righteous, but the Lord de-
livereth him out of them all. He keepeth all his
bones: not one of them is broken...The Lord re-
deemeth the soul of His servants: and none of
them that trust in Him shall be desolate."
(Psalm 34:19-20, 22).

Thus have I given you five lessons. Now let
me solemnly say that, with all the instruction
you may give to your children, you must always be deeply conscious that you are not capable of doing anything in the securing of the
child's salvation, but that it is God Himself
who, from the first to the last, must effect it
all. You are simply a pen: God can write with
you, but you cannot write anything by yourself. You are a sword: God can slay the child's
sin with you, but you cannot slay it of yourself.

Therefore, always be mindful of this, that
you must **first be taught of God yourself**.
Then you must ask God to use you to teach, for
unless a higher Teacher than you works with
you to instruct the child, the child must perish.
It is not your instruction that can save the
souls of your children; rather it is the blessing
of God the Holy Spirit accompanying and
blessing your labors.

May God bless and crown your efforts with
abundant success! He will surely do so if you
are instant in prayer, constant in supplication.
Never yet did the earnest teacher or preacher
"labour in vain, nor bring forth for trouble; for

thet are the seed of the blessed of the LORD" (Isaiah 65:23). Often has it been seen that bread cast upon the waters has been found after many days (see Ecclesiastes 11:1).

Chapter 13

Three Admonitions

Come, ye children, hearken unto me: I will
teach you the fear of the LORD.
—Psalm 34:11

First, recollect whom you are teaching; *"Come, ye children."* I think we ought always to have respect for our audience. I do not mean that we should care if we are preaching to Mr. So-and-So, Sir William this, or My Lord that, because in God's sight such titles are the merest trifles. Rather, we are to remember that we are preaching to men and women who have souls, so that we ought not to occupy their time by things that are not worth their hearing.

However, when you teach in Sunday schools, you are, if it is possible, in a more responsible situation even than a minister occupies. He preaches to grown-up people, to men of judgment, who, if they do not like what he preaches, can go somewhere else. But you teach children who have no option of going elsewhere. If you teach the child wrongly, he believes you. If you teach him heresies, he will receive them. What you teach him now, he will never forget.

You are not sowing, as some say, on virgin soil, for it has long been occupied by the devil. But you are sowing on a soil more fertile now than it ever will be again—soil that will produce fruit now, far better than it will do in later days. You are sowing on a young heart, and what you sow will be pretty sure to abide there, especially if you teach evil, for that will never be forgotten. You are beginning with the child. Take care what you do with him. Do not spoil him. Many a child has been treated like the Indian children who have copper plates put upon their foreheads, so that they may never grow.

There are many who are simpletons now, just because those who had the care of them when young gave them no opportunities of getting knowledge, so that, when they became old, they cared nothing about it. Have a care what you are doing. You are teaching children, so mind what you teach them. Put poison in the spring, and it will pollute the whole stream. Take care what you are doing! You are twisting the sapling, and the old oak will be bent thereby. Have a care, it is a child's soul you are tampering with, if you are tampering at all. It is a child's soul you are preparing for eternity, if God is with you. I give you a solemn admonition on every child's behalf. Surely, just as it is murder to administer poison to the dying, it must be far more criminal to give poison to the young life. If it is evil to mislead grey-headed age, it must be far more so to turn aside the feet of the young into the road of error, in which they may forever walk.

Secondly, recollect that you are teaching for God. *"Come, ye children, hearken unto me; I will teach you the fear of the Lord."* If you, as teachers, were only assembled to teach geography, it might not injure them eternally if you were to tell the children that the North Pole was close to the Equator; or if you were to say that the extremity of South America was very near the coast of Europe; or if you assured them that England was in the middle of Africa.

But you are not teaching geography, or astronomy, nor are you training the children for a business life in this world. You are, to the best of your ability, teaching them for God. You say to them, "Children, come here to be taught the Word of God. You come here, if it is possible, so that we may be the means of the salvation of your souls." Have a care what you are about when you pretend to be teaching them for God. Wound the child's hand if you will, but do not wound his heart for God's sake. Say whatever you like about temporal things; but, I beseech you, in spiritual matters, take care how you lead them.

Be careful that it is the truth which you inculcate, and only that. With such a responsibility, how solemn your work becomes! He who is doing a work for himself, may do it as he likes; but he who is laboring for another must take care to please his master. He who is employed by a monarch must beware how he performs his duty, but he who labors for God must tremble for fear that he may do his work poorly. Remember that you are laboring for God, if you are what you profess to be. Alas, I fear that many are far from having this serious view of the work of a Sunday-school teacher.

Third, remember that your children need teaching. *"Come, ye children, hearken unto me: I will teach you the fear of the Lord."* That makes your work all the more solemn. If children did not need teaching, I would not be so extremely anxious that you should teach them a right. Superfluous works, works that are not necessary, men may do as they please; but this work is absolutely necessary. Your child needs teaching. He was born in iniquity; in sin did his mother conceive him (see Psalm 51:5). He has an evil heart. He knows not God, and he never will know the Lord unless he is taught. He is not like some ground of which we have heard, that has good seed lying hidden in its very bowels. Instead, he has evil seed within his heart. God can place good seed there. You profess to be His instruments to scatter seed upon that child's heart. Remember, if that seed is not sown, he will be lost forever. His life will be a life of alienation from God; and at his death, everlasting punishment must be his portion.

Be careful, then, how you teach, remembering the urgent necessity of each case. This is not a house on fire, needing your assistance at the engine; nor is it a wreck at sea, demanding your oar in the lifeboat; but it is a deathless spirit calling aloud to you, "Come and help me." Therefore, I beseech you, teach the fear of the Lord, and that only. Be very anxious to say, and to say truly, *I will teach you the fear of the Lord.*

Chapter 14

The Psalmist's Invitation

Come, ye children, hearken unto me: I will teach you the fear of the LORD.
—Psalm 34:11

It is a singular thing that good men frequently discover their duty when they are placed in most humiliating positions. Never in David's life was he in a worse plight than that which suggested this Psalm. It is headed, *"A Psalm of David, when he changed his behavior before Abimelech; who drove him away, and he departed."* This poem was intended to commemorate that event, and was suggested by it.

David was carried before King Achish, the Abimelech of Philistia, and, in order to make his escape, he pretended to be mad, accompanying that profession of madness with certain very degrading actions which might well seem to signify his insanity. He was driven from the palace, and as usual, when such men are in the street, it is probable that a number of children assembled around him.

You have the sad story told in 1 Samuel 21:10-15. Whenever David sang songs of praise to Jehovah afterwards, recollecting how he had become the laughing-stock of little children, he seemed to say, "By my folly before the children in the streets, I have lowered myself in the estimation of generations that shall live after me; now I will endeavor to undo the mischief: *'Come, ye children, hearken unto me: I will teach you the fear of the Lord.'*"

Very possibly, if David had never been in such a position, he would never have thought of this duty. I do not discover that he ever said in any other psalm, *"Come, ye children, hearken unto me."* He had the cares of his cities, his provinces, and his nation pressing upon him, and may have been at other times very little attentive to the education of youth. But here, being brought into the meanest position man could possibly occupy, having become as one bereft of reason, he recollects his duty.

The exalted or prosperous Christian is not always mindful of "the lambs." That duty generally falls to the Peters, whose pride and confidence have been crushed, and who rejoice thus practically to answer their Lord's question, as the apostle did when Jesus said to him, *"Lovest thou Me?"* (John 21:15).

"Come, ye children, hearken unto me: I will teach you the fear of the Lord." The doctrine is, that children are capable of being taught the fear of the Lord.

Men are generally wisest after they have been most foolish. David had been extremely foolish, and now he became truly wise. Being so, it was not likely he would utter foolish sentiments or give directions such as would be dictated by a weak mind. We have heard it said by some that children cannot understand the mysteries of religion. We even know some teachers who cautiously avoid mentioning the great doctrines of the Gospel, because they think the children are not able to receive them.

Alas, the same mistake has crept into the pulpit! Among a certain group of preachers, it is currently believed that many of the doctrines of the Word of God, although true, are not fit to be taught to the people, since they would pervert them to their own destruction. Away with such priest craft! Whatever God has revealed ought to be preached. Whatever He has revealed, if I am not capable of understanding it, I will still believe and preach it. I do hold that there is no doctrine of the Word of God which a child, if he is capable of salvation, is not capable of receiving. I would have children taught all the great doctrines of truth without a solitary exception, that they may in their later days hold fast by them.

I can bear witness that children can understand the Scriptures. I am sure that, when I was but a child, I could have discussed many a knotty point of controversial theology, having heard both sides of the question freely stated among my father's circle of friends. In fact, children are capable of understanding some things in early life which we hardly understand as adults.

Children have eminently a simplicity of faith, and simplicity of faith is close to the highest knowledge. Indeed, we know not that there is much distinction between the simplicity of a child and the genius of the profoundest mind. He who receives things simply, as a child, will often have ideas which the man who is prone to make a logical course of thought of everything will never attain. If you wish to know whether children can be taught, I point you to many in our churches and in pious families—not prodigies, but such as we frequently see—Timothys and Samuels, and little girls, too, who have early come to know the Savior's love.

As soon as a child is capable of being lost, it is capable of being saved. As soon as a child can sin, that child can, if God's grace assists it, believe and receive the Word of God. As soon as children can learn evil, be assured that they are competent to learn good under the teaching of the Holy Spirit. Never go to your class with the thought that the children cannot comprehend you. If you do not make them understand, it is possibly because you do not yourselves understand. If you do not teach children what you wish them to learn, it may be because you are not fit for the task. You should find out simpler words, more fitted for their capacity. Then you would discover that it was not the fault of the child, but the fault of the teacher if the child did not learn.

I firmly believe that children are capable of salvation. He who, in divine sovereignty, reclaimed the grey-haired sinner from the error of his ways, can turn a little child from his youthful follies. He who, in the eleventh hour, finds some standing idle in the market place and sends them into the vineyard, can and does call men at the dawning of the day to labor for Him. He who can change the course of a river when it has swelled and has become a mighty flood, can control a new-born rivulet leaping from its cradle fountain and make it run into the channel He desires. He can do all things. He can work upon children's hearts as He pleases, for all are under His control.

I will not pause to establish the doctrine, because I do not consider that any are so foolish as to doubt it. But, although you believe it, I fear many do not expect to hear of children being saved. Throughout the churches, I have noticed a kind of abhorrence of anything which resembles child piety. We are frightened at the idea of a little boy loving Christ. If we hear of a little girl following the Savior, we say it is a youthful fancy, an early impression that will die away. I beseech you, never treat child piety with suspicion. It is a tender plant; do not brush it too hard.

I heard a tale, some time ago, which I believe to be perfectly authentic. A dear little girl, some five or six years old, a true lover of Jesus, requested of her mother that she might join the church. The mother told her she was too young, and the poor little thing was exceedingly grieved. After a while, the mother, who saw that piety was in her child's heart, spoke to the minister on the subject. The minister talked to the child, and said to the mother, "I am thoroughly convinced of her piety, but I cannot take her into the church, she is too young." When the child heard that, a strange gloom passed over her face. The next morning, when the mother went to her little bed, she lay with a pearly tear on each eye, dead from grief. Her heart was broken because she could not follow her Savior and do as He had bidden her. I would not have murdered that child for the world! Take care how you treat youthful devotion. Be very tender in dealing with it.

Believe that children can be saved just as much as yourselves. I do most firmly believe in the salvation of children. When you see the young heart brought to the Savior, do not stand by and speak harshly, mistrusting everything. It is better sometimes to be deceived than to be the means of offending one of these little ones who believe in Jesus. May God send to His people a firm belief that little buds of grace are worthy of all tender care!

Chapter 15

King David's Two Encouragements

*Come, ye children, hearken unto me: I will
teach you the fear of the LORD.*
—Psalm 34:11

The first encouragement is that of a pious
example. David said, *"Come, ye children,
hearken unto me: I will teach you the fear of the
Lord."* You are not ashamed to tread in the
footsteps of David, are you? You will not object
to follow the example of one who was first
eminently holy and then eminently great.
Shall the shepherd boy, the giant slayer, the
sweet psalmist of Israel, the mighty monarch,
leave footprints in which you are too proud to
tread? Ah, no! You will be happy, I am sure, to
be as David was.

If you want, however, a higher example
even than that of David, hear the Son of David
while from His lips flow the sweet words,

"Suffer the little children to come unto Me, and forbid them not, for of such is the kingdom of God" (Mark 10:14). I am sure it would encourage you if you always thought of these examples.

You who are teaching children are not dishonored by that occupation. Some may say, "You are only a Sunday-school teacher," but you are a noble personage, holding an honorable office, and having illustrious predecessors. We love to see people of some standing in society take an interest in Sunday schools. One great fault in many of our churches is that the children are left for the young people to care for. The older members, who have more wisdom, take very little notice of them. Very often, the wealthier members of the church stand aside as if the teaching of the poor were not (as indeed it is) the special business of the rich.

I hope for the day when the mighty men of Israel will be found helping in this great warfare against the enemy. In the United States we have heard of Presidents, of Judges, Members of Congress, and persons in the highest positions, not condescending (I scorn to use such a term), but honoring themselves by teaching little children in Sunday schools. He who teaches a class in a Sunday school has earned a good title. I had rather receive the degree of S.S.T. than MA., B.A., or any other honor that ever was conferred by men. Let me beg you to take heart, because your duties are so honorable. Let the royal example of David and the holy example of Jesus Christ inspire you with fresh diligence and increasing ardor, with confident and enduring perseverance. Continue on in your blessed work, saying as David did, *"Come, ye children, hearken unto me: I will teach you the fear of the Lord."*

The second is the encouragement of great success. David said, *"Come, ye children, hearken unto me."* He did not include, "perhaps..." but definitely said, *"I **will** teach you."* He knew he had success and that others would also have. The success of Sunday schools! If I begin on that, I will have an endless theme; therefore, I will not commence. Many volumes might be written on it, and then when all were written, we might say, "I suppose that even the world itself could not contain all that might be written."

In heaven, where the starry hosts perpetually sing God's high praises, up where the white-robed throng cast their crowns before His feet, we will behold the success of Sunday schools. There, too, where infant millions assemble Sunday after Sunday to sing, "Gentle Jesus, meek and mild," we see with joy the success of Sunday schools.

And here, in almost every pulpit of our land, and there in the pews where the deacons sit and godly members join in worship, the success of Sunday schools can be seen. Far away across the broad ocean, in the islets of the South Pacific and in all lands where those dwell who bow before blocks of wood and stone, there are the missionaries who were saved in Sunday schools. The thousands, blessed by their labors, contribute to swell the mighty stream of the incalculable, infinite success of Sunday-school instruction.

Go on with your holy service. Much has been done already, but more will yet be done. Let all your past victories inflame you with fresh ardor. Let the remembrance of your triumphs in previous campaigns and all trophies won for your Savior on the battlefield of the past be your encouragement to press on with the duty of the present and the future.

Chapter 16

Childhood and Holy Scripture

But continue thou in the things which thou hast learned and hast been assured of, knowing of whom thou hast learned them; And that from a child thou hast known the holy scriptures, which are able to make thee wise unto salvation through faith which is in Christ Jesus.
—2 Timothy 3:14-15

Paul himself taught young Timothy the Gospel. He made him not only hear his doctrine, but see his practice. We cannot force truth on men, but we can make our teaching clear and decided, and make our lives consistent with our words. Truth and holiness are the surest antidotes to error and unrighteousness. Paul said to Timothy, *"Continue thou in the things which thou hast learned and hast* *been assured of, knowing of whom thou hast learned them."*

Paul then dwelt on another potent remedy which had been of great service to the young preacher—namely, the knowing of the Holy Scriptures from his earliest childhood. This was to young Timothy one of his best safeguards. His early training held him like an anchor, and saved him from the dreadful drift of the age. Happy young man, of whom the apostle could say, *"From a child thou hast known the Holy Scriptures, which are able to make thee wise unto salvation through faith which is in Christ Jesus"*!

To be prepared for the coming conflict, we have not only to preach and to live the Gospel, but also to take care that we teach the children the Word of the Lord. This last is especially to be attended to, for it is by *"the mouth of babes and sucklings"* (Psalm 8:2) that God will still the enemy.

It is idle to dream that human learning must be met by human learning, or that Satan must cast out Satan. No! Lift up the brazen serpent wherever the fiery serpents are biting the people, and men shall look to it and live (see Numbers 21:8-9). Bring the children out, hold them up, and turn their little eyes towards the divinely ordained remedy. Still there is life in a look—life as against the varied venoms of the serpent which are now poisoning the blood of men. There is no cure after all for midnight but the rising sun. No hope remains for a dark world but in that light which lightens every man. Shine forth, O Sun of Righteousness, and mist, and cloud, and darkness must disappear.

Teachers, keep to the apostolic plans and be assured of apostolic success. Preach Christ; preach the Word in season and out of season (see 2 Timothy 4:2); and teach the children. One of God's chief methods for preserving His fields from tares is to sow them early with wheat.

The work of God's grace in Timothy commenced with early instruction: *"From a child thou hast known the Holy Scriptures."* Note **the time for instruction**. The expression, *"from a child,"* might be better understood if we read it, "from a very child;" or, as the Revised Version has it, *"from a babe."* It does not mean a well-grown child or youth, but a child just rising out of infancy. From a very child, Timothy had known the sacred writings. This expression is, no doubt, used to show that we cannot begin too early to permeate the minds of our children with scriptural knowledge.

Babes receive impressions long before we are aware of the fact. During the first months of a child's life, it learns more than we imagine. It soon learns the love of its mother and its own dependence. If the mother is wise, it learns the meaning of obedience and the necessity of yielding its will to a higher will. This may be the keynote of its whole future life. If the babe learns obedience and submission early, it may save a thousand tears from the child's eyes, and as many from the mother's heart. A special advantage is lost when even babyhood is left uncultured.

The Holy Scriptures may be learned by children as soon as they are capable of understanding anything. A remarkable fact, which I have heard asserted by many teachers, is that children learn to read from the Bible better than from any other book. I scarcely know why. It may, perhaps, be due to the simplicity of the language. But whatever the reason, I believe it is so. A biblical fact will often be grasped when an incident of common history is forgotten.

There is an adaptation in the Bible for human beings of all ages, and therefore it has a fitness for children. We make a mistake when we think that we must begin with something else and lead up to the Scriptures. The Bible is the book for the dawn of day. Parts of it are beyond a child's mind, for they are above the comprehension of the most advanced among us. There are depths in it in which leviathan may swim; but there are also brooks in which a lamb may wade. Wise teachers know how to lead their little ones into the green pastures beside the still waters.

I was noticing that in the life of that man of God whose loss presses very heavily upon many of our hearts—namely, the Earl of Shaftesbury—that his first religious impressions were produced by a humble woman. The impressions which made Shaftesbury the man of God, and the friend of man, were received in the nursery. Little Lord Ashley had a godly nurse who spoke to him of the things of God. He tells us that she died before he was seven years of age—clear proof that early in life his heart had been able to receive the seal of the Spirit of God and to receive it by humble instrumentality. Blessed among women was she whose name we know not, but who worked incalculable service for God and man by her holy teaching of the chosen child. Young nurses, note this.

Give us the first seven years of a child, with God's grace, and we may defy the world, the flesh, and the devil to ruin that immortal soul. Those first years, when the clay is yet soft and plastic, go far to decide the form of the vessel. Do not say that your office, you who teach the young, is in the least degree inferior to ours, whose main business is with older folks. No, you have the first chance with these precious young souls. The impressions you make, since they come first, will endure to the last. I pray that they may be good, and only good!

Among the thoughts that come to an old man before he enters heaven, the most plentiful are those that had before visited him when he sat upon his mother's knee. That which made Dr. Guthrie ask for a "bairn's hymn" when he was dying, is but an instinct of our nature, which leads us to complete the circle by folding together the ends of life. Childlike things are dearest to old age. We shuffle off a portion of the coil that surrounds and hampers us, and go back again to our more natural selves. Therefore, the old songs are on our lips, and the old thoughts are in our minds. The teachings of our childhood leave clean-cut and sharp impressions upon the mind, which remain after seventy years have passed. Let us see that such impressions are made for the highest ends.

It is well to note **the admirable selection of instructors**. We are not at a loss to tell who instructed youthful Timothy. In this epistle Paul says, *"When I call to remembrance the unfeigned faith that is in thee, which dwelt first in thy grandmother Lois, and thy mother Eunice; and I am persuaded that in thee also"* (2 Timothy 1:5). No doubt grandmother Lois and mother Eunice united in teaching the little one. Who should teach the children but the parents? Timothy's father was a Greek, and probably a heathen, but this child was happy in having a venerable grandmother, so often the dearest of all relatives to a little child. He was blessed also with a gracious mother, once a devout Jewess, and afterwards also a firmly believing Christian, who made it her daily pleasure to teach her own dear child the Word of the Lord.

O dear mothers, please understand that you have **a very sacred trust** reposed in you by God! He has in effect said unto you, *"Take this child away, and nurse it for Me, and I will give thee thy wages"* (Exodus 2:9). You are called to equip the future man of God, that he may be *"thoroughly furnished unto all good works"* (2 Timothy 3:17). If God spares you, you may live to hear that pretty boy speak to thousands, and you will have the sweet reflection in your heart that the quiet teachings of the nursery led the adult man to love his God and serve Him.

Those who think that a woman detained at home by her little family is doing nothing, think the reverse of what is true. Scarcely can the godly mother quit her home for a place of worship. However, dream not that she is lost to the work of the church. Far from it, she is doing the best possible service for her Lord.

Mothers, **the godly training of your offspring is your first and most pressing duty**. Christian women, by teaching children the Holy Scriptures, are as much fulfilling their part for the Lord as Moses did in judging Israel, or Solomon in building the temple.

Chapter 17

Witnesses Converted in Youth

*And it shall come to pass, as soon as I am gone
from thee, that the spirit of the LORD shall
carry thee whither I know not; and so when I
come and tell Ahab, and he cannot find thee, he
shall slay me: but I thy servant
fear the LORD from my youth.*
—1 Kings 18:12

I suspect that Elijah did not think very much
of Obadiah. He does not treat him with any
great consideration, but addresses him more
sharply than one would expect from a fellow
believer. Elijah was the man of action—bold,
always in the front, with nothing to conceal.
Obadiah was a quiet believer, true and stead-
fast, but in a very difficult position, and therefore driven to perform his duty in a less open
manner. His faith in the Lord swayed his life,
but did not drive him out of the court.

I notice that even after Elijah had learned more of him at this interview, he speaks concerning God's people as if he did not reckon much about Obadiah and others like him. He says, *"They have thrown down Thine altars, and slain Thy prophets with the sword; and I, even I only, am left; and they seek my life, to take it away"* (1 Kings 19:10). He knew very well that Obadiah was left, who, though not exactly a prophet, was a man of mark. However, Elijah seems to ignore him as if he were of small account in the great struggle. I suppose it was because this man of iron, this prophet of fire and thunder, this mighty servant of the Most High, set small store by anybody who did not come to the front and fight like himself.

I know it is the tendency of brave and zealous minds somewhat to undervalue quiet, retiring piety. True and accepted servants of God may be doing their best under great disadvantages against fierce opposition, but they may scarcely be known, and may even shun the least recognition. Therefore, men who live in the fierce light of public life are apt to underestimate them. These minor stars are lost in the brilliance of the man whom God lights up like a new sun to flame through the darkness. Elijah flashed over the sky of Israel like a thunderbolt from the hand of the Eternal, and naturally he would be somewhat impatient with those whose movements were slower and less conspicuous. It is Martha and Mary over again, in some respects.

The Lord does not love that His servants, however great they are, should think lightly of their less prominent comrades. It occurs to me that He so arranged matters that Obadiah became important to Elijah when he had to face the wrathful king of Israel. The prophet is bidden to go and show himself to Ahab, and he does so; but he judges that it would be better to begin by showing himself to the governor of his palace, so that Obadiah may break the news to his master and prepare him for the interview. Ahab was exasperated by the terrible results of the long drought, and might in his sudden fury attempt to kill the prophet. Thus Ahab is to have time for consideration, that he may cool down a little.

Elijah has an interview with Obadiah, and bids him to go and say to Ahab, *"Behold Elijah is here"* (1 Kings 18:8). It may sometimes be the nearest way to our object to go a little round about. But it is remarkable that Obadiah should thus be made useful to a man so much his superior. He who never feared the face of kings, nevertheless, found himself using as his helper a far more timid individual.

We learn further from the narrative that God will never leave Himself without witnesses in this world, and He will not leave

Himself without witnesses in the worst places of the world. What a horrible abode for a true believer Ahab's court must have been! If there had been no sinner there but that woman Jezebel, she was enough to make the place a cesspool of iniquity. That strong-minded, proud, Sidonian Queen twisted poor Ahab around her finger just as she pleased. He might never have been the persecutor he was if his wife had not stirred him up. But she hated the worship of Jehovah intensely and despised the homeliness of Israel in comparison with the more pompous style of Sidon. Ahab must yield to her imperious demands, for she would brook no contradiction. When her proud spirit was roused, she defied all opposition. Yet in that very court where Jezebel was mistress, the chamberlain was a man who feared God greatly. Never be surprised to meet with a believer anywhere. Grace can live where you would never have expected to see it survive for an hour.

Joseph feared God in the court of Pharaoh, Daniel was a trusted counselor of Nebuchadnezzar, Mordecai waited at the gate of Ahasuerus, Pilate's wife pleaded for the life of Jesus, and there were saints in Caeser's household. Think of finding diamonds of the first quality on such a dunghill as Nero's palace. Those who feared God in Rome were not only Christians, but they were examples to all other Christians for their brotherly love and generosity. Surely there is no place in this land where there is not some light. The darkest cavern of iniquity has its torch. Do not be afraid. You may find followers of Jesus in the precincts of pandemonium. In the palace of Ahab you meet an Obadiah who rejoices to hold fellowship with despised saints, and quits the receptions of a monarch for the hiding places of persecuted ministers.

I notice that these witnesses for God are very often people converted in their youth. He seems to take a delight to make these His special standard-bearers in the day of battle. Look at Samuel! When all Israel became disgusted with the wickedness of Eli's sons, the child Samuel ministered before the Lord. Look at David! When he was but a shepherd boy, he wakes the echoes of the lone hills with his psalms and the accompanying music of his harp. See Josiah! When Israel had revolted, it was a child, Josiah by name, that broke down the altars of Baal and burned the bones of his priests. Daniel was but a youth when he took his stand for purity and God.

The Lord has today—I know not where— some little Luther on his mother's knee, some young Calvin learning in our Sunday school, some youthful Zwingle singing a hymn to Jesus. This age may grow worse and worse. I sometimes think it will, for many signs look that way, but the Lord is preparing for it. The days are dark and ominous. This eventide may darken down into a blacker night than has been known before, but God's cause is safe in God's hands. His work will not tarry for lack of men. Put not forth the hand of Uzzah to steady the ark of the Lord. It will go safely on in God's predestined way. Christ will not fail nor be discouraged. God buries His workmen, but His work lives on. If there is not in the palace a king who honors God, there shall yet be found there a governor who fears the Lord from his youth, who will take care of the Lord's prophets and hide them away until better days come.

Therefore, be of good courage, and look for happier hours. Nothing of real value is in jeopardy because Jehovah is on the throne! The Lord's reserves are coming, and their drums beat victory.

Chapter 18

Obadiah's Early Piety

I thy servant fear the Lord from my youth.
—1 Kings 18:12

Obadiah possessed devotion from his early years. Oh, that all our youth who may grow up to manhood and womanhood may be able to say the same! Happy are the people who are in such a state!

How Obadiah came to fear the Lord in youth we cannot tell. The instructor by whom he was led to faith in Jehovah is not mentioned. Yet we may reasonably conclude that he had believing parents. Slender as the ground may seem to be, I think it is pretty firm, when I remind you of his name. This would very naturally be given him by his father or his mother, and as it signifies "the servant of Jehovah," I should think that name indicated his parents' piety. In the days when there was persecution everywhere against the faithful, and the name of Jehovah was in contempt because the calves of Bethel and the images of Baal were set up everywhere, I do not think that unbelieving parents would have given their child the name, "the servant of Jehovah," if they themselves had not felt a reverence for the Lord. They would not idly have courted the remarks of their idolatrous neighbors and the scorn of the great. In a time and culture in which names had special meanings, they would have called him "the child of Baal," or "the servant of Chemosh," or some other name expressive of reverence to the popular gods, if the fear of God had not been before their eyes.

The selection of such a name betrays to me their earnest desire that their boy might grow up to serve Jehovah, and never bow his knee before the abhorred idols of the Sidonian queen. Whether this is so or not, it is quite certain that thousands of the most intelligent believers owe their first bent toward godliness to the sweet associations of home. How many of us might well have borne some such a name as that of Obadiah, for no sooner did we see the light than our parents tried to enlighten us with the truth. We were consecrated to the service of God before we knew that there was a God. Many a tear of earnest prayer fell on our infant brows and sealed us for heaven. We were nursed in the atmosphere of devotion.

There was scarcely a day in which we were not urged to be faithful servants of God, and entreated while we were yet young to seek Jesus and give our hearts to Him.

If he had no gracious parents, I cannot tell how Obadiah came to be a believer in the Lord in those sad days, unless he fell in with some kind teacher, tender nurse, or perhaps good servant in his father's house or pious neighbor, who dared to gather little children round about him and tell of the Lord God of Israel. Some holy woman may have instilled the law of the Lord into his young mind before the priests of Baal could poison him with their falsehoods. No mention is made of anybody in connection with this man's conversion in his youth, and it does not matter, does it? You and I do not want to be mentioned if we are right-hearted servants of God.

This early piety of Obadiah's had special marks of genuineness about it. The way in which he described it is very instructive, *"I thy servant fear the Lord from my youth."* I hardly remember in all my life to have heard the piety of children described in ordinary conversation by this term, though it is the common word of the Scriptures. We say, "The dear child loved God." We talk of their being made happy and so forth. I do not question the rightness of the language. Still, the Holy Spirit speaks of *"the fear of the Lord"* as *"the beginning of wisdom"*

(Proverbs 9:10). David says, *"Come, ye children, hearken unto me: I will teach you the fear of the Lord"* (Psalm 34:11). Children will get great joy through faith in the Lord Jesus; but that joy, if true, is full of lowly reverence and awe of the Lord.

You do not need me to speak to you extensively on the advantages of early piety. I will, therefore, only sum them up in a few sentences. To be a believer in God early in life is to be saved from a thousand regrets. Such a man will never have to say that he carries in his bones the sins of his youth. Early piety helps us to form associations for the rest of life which will prove helpful, and it saves us from those which are harmful.

The Christian young man will not fall into the common sins of young men and injure his constitution by excesses. He will be likely to be married to a Christian woman, and so to have a holy companion in his march toward heaven. He will select as his associates those who will be his friends in the church and not in the tavern; his helpers in virtue, and not his tempters to vice. Depend upon it, a great deal depends upon whom we choose for our companions when we begin life. If we start in bad company, it is very hard to break away from it.

The man brought to Christ early in life has this further advantage, that he is helped to form holy habits, and he is saved from being the slave of their opposites. Habits soon become a second nature. To form new ones is hard work, but those formed in youth remain in old age. There is something in that verse:

> " 'Tis easier work if we begin
>   To serve the Lord be times;
> But sinners who grow old in sin
>   Are hardened in their crimes."

I am sure it is so. Moreover, I notice that, very frequently, those who are brought to Christ while young grow in grace more rapidly and readily than others do. They have not so much to unlearn, and they have not such a heavy weight of old memories to carry. The scars and bleeding sores which come of having spent years in the service of the devil are missed by those whom the Lord brings into His church before they have wandered far into the world.

As to early piety in its bearing upon others, I cannot recommend it too highly. How attractive it is! Grace looks loveliest in youth. That which would not be noticed in the grown-up man, strikes at once the most careless observer when seen in a child. Grace in a child has a convincing force: the infidel drops his weapon and admires. A word spoken by a child abides in the memory, and its artless accents touch the heart. Where the minister's sermon fails, the child's prayer may gain the victory.

Moreover, religious belief in a child suggests encouragement to those of riper years. Others, seeing the little one saved, say to themselves, "Why should not we also find the Lord?" By a certain secret power, it opens closed doors and turns the key in the lock of unbelief. Where nothing else could win a way for truth, a child's love has done it. It is still true, *"Out of the mouth of babes and sucklings hast Thou ordained strength because of Thine enemies, that Thou mightest still the enemy and the avenger"* (Psalm 8:2).

Chapter 19

Obadiah and Elijah

I thy servant fear the Lord from my youth.
—1 Kings 18:3

Youthful piety leads to persevering piety. Obadiah could say, *"I thy servant fear the Lord from my youth."* Time had not changed him: whatever his age may have been, his religion had not decayed. We are all fond of novelty, and I have known some men to go wrong, as it were, for a change. It is not burning quick to the death in martyrdom that is the hard work; roasting before a slow fire is a far more terrible test of spiritual mettle. To continue in grace during a long life of temptation is to be gracious indeed. For the grace of God to convert a man like Paul, who was full of threatenings against the saints, is a great marvel. But for the grace of God to preserve a believer for ten, twenty, thirty, forty, fifty or more years is quite as great a miracle and deserves more of our praise than it usually commands. Obadiah was not affected by the lapse of time: when he was old, he was found to be what he was when young.

Nor was he carried away by the fashion of those evil times. To be a servant of Jehovah was thought to be a mean thing, old-fashioned, ignorant, a thing of the past. The worship of Baal was the "modern thought" of the hour. All the court walked after the god of Sidon, and all the courtiers went in the same way. My lord and my lady worshipped Baal, for the Queen worshipped Baal. But Obadiah said, *"I thy servant fear Jehovah from my youth."* Blessed is the man who cares nothing for the fashion, for it passes away. If for a while it rages towards evil, what can the believing man do but abide steadfastly by the right?

Obadiah was not even affected by the absence of the means of grace. The priests and Levites had fled into Judah, the prophets had been killed or hidden away, and there was no public worship of Jehovah in Israel. The temple was far away at Jerusalem. Therefore, he had no opportunity of hearing anything that could strengthen him or stimulate him, yet he held on his way.

Added to this, there were the difficulties of his position. He was chamberlain of the palace. If he had pleased Jezebel and worshipped Baal, he might have found it easier in his situation, for he would have enjoyed her royal patronage. But there he was, governor in Ahab's house, and yet fearing Jehovah. He must have had to walk very delicately and watch his words most carefully. I do not wonder that he became a very cautious person and was a little afraid even of Elijah, for fear that he was giving him a commission which would lead to his destruction. He came to be extremely prudent. He looked on things round about so as neither to compromise his conscience nor jeopardize his position. It requires an uncommonly wise man to do that, but he who can accomplish it is to be commended. He did not run away from his position, nor retreat from his religion. If he had been forced to do wrong, I am sure he would have imitated the priests and Levites and have fled into Judah, where the worship of Jehovah continued. But he felt that he could do something for God in his advantageous position without yielding to idolatry. Therefore, he determined to stop and fight it out.

When there is no hope of victory, you may as well retire. But brave is the man who, when the bugle sounds retreat, does not hear it, who puts his blind eye to the telescope and cannot see the signal to cease firing, but just holds his position against all odds, and does all the damage he can to the enemy. Obadiah was a man who did in truth "hold the fort," for he felt that when all the prophets were doomed by

Jezebel, it was his part to stay near the tigress and save the lives of at least a hundred servants of God from her cruel power. If he could not do more, at least he would not have lived in vain if he accomplished that much.

I admire the man whose decision was equal to his prudence, though I would greatly fear to occupy so perilous a place. His course was something like walking on the tightrope with Blondin. I would not like to try it myself, nor would I recommend any of you to attempt a feat so difficult. The part of Elijah is much safer and grander. The prophet's course was plain enough. He did nnot have to please, but to reprove Ahab. His path was not to be wary, but to act in a bold, outspoken manner for the God of Israel.

How much the greater man Elijah seems to be when the two stand together in the scene before us. Obidiah falls on his face and calls him *"My lord Elijah."* Well Obadiah might, for he was far his inferior. Yet I must not fall morally into Elijah's attitude myself, lest I have to pull myself up with a sharp check. It was a great thing for Obadiah that he could manage Ahab's household with Jezebel in it, and yet, for all that, win this commendation from the Spirit of God that he feared the Lord greatly.

He persevered, too, notwithstanding his success in life. That I hold to be much to his credit. There is nothing more perilous to a man than to prosper in this world and become rich and respectable. Of course we desire it, wish for it, strive for it; but how many in winning it have lost all as to spiritual wealth! The man used to love the people of God, and now he says, "They are a vulgar class of persons." So long as he could hear the Gospel, he did not mind the architecture of the house; but now he has grown aesthetic and must have a spire, Gothic architecture, a marble pulpit, priestly millinery, a conservatory in the church, and all sorts of pretty things. As he has filled his pocket, he has emptied his brains, and especially emptied his heart. He has gotten away from truth and principle in proportion to the advances he has made in his estate.

This is a mean business, which at one time he would have been the first to condemn. There is no chivalry in such conduct. It is dastardly to the last degree. God save us from it. But a great many people are not saved from it. Their religion is not a matter of principle, but a matter of interest. It is not the pursuit of truth, but a hankering after society, whatever that may mean. It is not their object to glorify God, but to get rich husbands for their girls. It is not conscience that guides them, but the hope of being able to invite Sir John to dinner with them, and of dining at the Great Hall in return.

Do not think I am sarcastic. I speak in sober sadness of things which make one feel ashamed. I hear of them daily, though they do not personally affect me. This is an age of meannesses disguised under the notion of respectability. God send us men of the stuff of John Knox, or, if you prefer it, of the adamantine metal of Elijah. If these should prove too stiff and stern, we could even be content with such men as Obadiah. Possibly these might be harder to produce than Elijahs, but *"with God all things are possible"* (Matthew 19:26).

Obadiah, with his early grace and persevering decision, became a man of eminent piety. This is the more remarkable considering what he was and where he was. Eminent piety in a Lord High Chamberlain of Ahab's court! This is a wonder of grace indeed. This man's religion was intense within him. If he did not make the open use of it that Eliajah did, he was not called to such a career. Nevertheless, it dwelt deep within his soul, and others knew it. I have no doubt whatsoever that Jezebel knew it. She did not like him, but she had to endure him. She looked askance at him, but she could not dislodge him. Ahab had learned to trust him and could not do without him, for he probably furnished him with a little strength of mind. Possibly Ahab liked to retain him just to show Jezebel that he could be obstinate if he liked, and was still a man.

Account for it how you may, it is unique that, in this center of rebellion against God, there was one whose devotion to God was intense. As it is horrible to find a Judas among the apostles, so it is grand to discover an Obadiah among Ahab's courtiers. What grace must have been at work to maintain such a fire in the midst of the sea, such godliness in the midst of the vilest iniquity!

Obadiah's early religion became comfortable piety to him afterwards. When he thought Elijah was about to expose him to great danger, he pleaded his long service of God, saying, *"I thy servant fear the Lord from my youth"*; just as David, when he grew old, said, *"O God, Thou hast taught me from my youth: and hitherto have I declared Thy wondrous works; now also when I am old and greyheaded, O God, forsake me not"* (Psalm 71:17-18).

It will be a great comfort to people, when old, to look back upon a life spent in the service of God. You will not trust in it, you will not think that there is any merit in it, but you will bless God for it. A servant who has been with his master from his youth ought not to be turned adrift when he grows grey. A right-minded master respects the person who has served him long and well. Suppose you had living in the family an old nurse who had nursed you when you were a child and had lived to bring up your children, would you turn

153

her into the street when she was past her work? No, you would do your best for her. If it is in your power you will keep her out of the workhouse. Now, the Lord is much more kind and gracious than we are, and He will never turn away His old servants.

Chapter 20

Abijah's "Some Good Thing"

And all Israel shall mourn for him, and bury him: for he only of Jeroboam shall come to the grave, because in him there is found some good thing toward the LORD God of Israel in the house of Jeroboam.
—1 Kings 14:13

J eroboam had proved false to the Lord who had placed him upon the throne of Israel, and the time had come for his overthrow. The Lord, who usually brings forth the rod before He lifts the axe, sent sickness into his house: his son Abijah was extremely sick. Then the parents remembered an old prophet of God and desired to know through him what would happen to the child.

Fearful lest the prophet should pronounce plagues upon him and his child if he knew that the inquirer was the wife of Jeroboam, the king begged the Egyptian princess whom he had married to disguise herself as a farmer's wife, to get from the man of God a more favorable answer. Poor foolish king, to imagine that a prophet who could see into futurity could not also see through any disguise with which his queen might surround herself! So anxious was the mother to know the fate of her son, that she left his sick chamber to go to Shiloh to hear the sentence of the prophet. Vain was her clever disguise! The blind prophet was still a seer, and not only discerned her before she entered the house, but saw the future of her family. She came full of superstition to be told her fortune, but she went away heavy, having been told her faults and her doom.

In the terrible tidings which the prophet Ahijah delivered to this wife of Jeroboam, there was only one bright spot, only one word of solace. I am greatly afraid that it gave no kind of comfort to the heathen queen. The child was mercifully appointed to die, for in him there was *"found some good thing toward Jehovah, God of Israel."*

We are going to look into the little that we know of the young prince Abijah. His name was a suitable one. A good name may belong to a very bad man, but in this case a gracious name was worthily worn. He called God his *Father*, and his name signifies that fact. *Ab*, you know, is the word for Father, and *Jah* is

Jehovah—Jehovah was his Father. I would not have mentioned the name had not his life made it true. Oh, you who bear good Bible names, see that you do not dishonor them!

There was in this child *"some good thing toward the Lord God of Israel,"* but what was it? Who can define it? A boundless field for conjecture opens before us. We know there was in him some good thing, but what form that took we do not know. Tradition has made assertions, but as these are mere inventions to fill a gap, they are scarcely worth mentioning. Probably, our own reflections will be as near the mark as these improbable traditions.

We may learn much from the silence of Scripture. We are not told precisely what the good thing was, because **any good thing towards the Lord is a sufficient sign of grace**. Though the child's faith is not mentioned, we are sure that he had faith in the living God, since without it nothing in him would have been good towards God, for *"without faith it is impossible to please God."* He was a child believer in Jehovah, the God of Israel. Perhaps his mother left him at his own request to go to the Lord's prophet for him. Many false prophets were around the palace. His father might not have sent to Shiloh had not the boy pleaded for it. The child believed in the great invisible God who made the heavens and the earth, and he worshipped Him in faith.

However, I would not wonder if, in that child, his love was more apparent than his faith. Converted children more usually talk of loving Christ than they do of trusting in Him, not because faith is not in them, but because the emotion of love is more congenial to the child's nature than the more intellectual act of faith. The heart is large in the child, and therefore love becomes his most conspicuous fruit. I have no doubt this child showed an early affection towards the unseen Jehovah, and a distaste for the idols of his father's court. Possibly he displayed a holy horror of the worship of God under the figure of a calf. Even a child would have intelligence enough to perceive that it must be wrong to liken the great and glorious God to a bullock which has horns and hoofs. Perhaps the child's refined nature also started back from those base priests of the lowest of the land whom his father had raked together. We do not know exactly the form it took, but there it was: *"some good thing"* was in the child's heart towards Jehovah, God of Israel.

It was not merely a good inclination which was in him, nor a good desire, but a really good, substantial virtue. There was in him a true and substantial existence of grace, far more than a transient desire. What child is there that has not at some time or other, if it has been trained in the fear of God, felt tremblings of heart and desires towards God? Such goodness is as common as the early dew; but, alas, it passes away quite as speedily. The young Abijah possessed something within him sufficiently real and substantial to be called a *"good thing."* The Spirit of God had worked a sure work in him, and left within him a priceless jewel of grace. Let us admire this good thing, though we cannot precisely describe it.

Let us admire, also, that this *"some good thing"* should have been in the child's heart, for its entrance is unknown. We cannot tell how grace entered the palace of Tirzah and gained this youthful heart. God saw the good thing, for He sees the least good thing in any of us, since He has a quick eye to perceive anything that looks toward Himself. But how did this gracious work come to the child? We are not told, and this silence is a lesson to us. It is not essential for us to know how a child receives grace.

We need not be painfully anxious about having to know when, where, or how a child is converted. It may be impossible to tell, for the work may have been so gradual that day and hour cannot be known. Even those who are converted in riper years cannot all describe their conversion in detail. Much less can we expect to map the experience of children who have never gone into outward sin, but under the restraints of godly education have kept the commandments from their youth up, like the young man in the gospel narrative.

How came this child to have this good thing in his heart? So far we know it exists. We are sure that God placed it there, but by what means? The child, in all probability, did not hear the teaching of the prophets of God. He was never, like young Samuel, taken up to the house of the Lord. His mother was an idolatrous princess, his father was among the most wicked of men, and yet the grace of God reached their child.

Did the Spirit of the Lord operate upon his heart through his own thoughts? Did he think over the matter, and did he come to the conclusion that God was God, and that He must not be worshipped as his father worshipped Him, under the image of a calf? Even a child might see this. Had some hymn to Jehovah been sung under the palace wall by some lone worshipper? Had the child seen his father on that day when he lifted up his hand against the prophet of Jehovah at the altar of Bethel, when suddenly his right hand withered at his side? Did the tears start from the boy's eye when he saw his father thus paralyzed in the arm of his strength? And did he laugh for very joy of heart when, by the prophet's prayer, his father was restored again? Did that great miracle of mercy cause him to love the God of Israel? Is it a mere fancy that this may have been so? A withered right hand in a father, and that father a king, is a thing a child is pretty sure to be told of. And if it is restored by prayer, the wonder would naturally fill the palace and be spoken of by everybody, and the prince would hear of it.

What if this little child had a godly nurse? What if some girl like she that waited upon Naaman's wife was the messenger of love to him? As she carried him to and fro, did his nurse sing him one of the songs of Zion and tell him of Joseph and Samuel? Israel had not yet so long forsaken her God as to be without many a faithful follower of the God of Abraham. Perhaps by one of these sufficient knowledge was conveyed to the child to become the means of conveying the love of God to his soul.

We may conjecture, but we may not pretend to be sure that it was so, nor is there any need that we should. If the sun is risen, it matters little when the day first dawned. Be it ours when we see in children *"some good thing"* to rest content with that truth, even if we cannot tell how it came there. God's electing love is never short of means to carry out its purpose. He can send His grace into the heart of Jeroboam's family. While the father is prostrate before his idols, the Lord can find a true worshipper for Himself in the king's child. *"Out of the mouths of babes and sucklings hast Thou ordained strength because of Thine enemies."*

Your footsteps are not always seen, O God of grace, but we have learned to adore You in Your work, even when we discern not Your way.

This *"good thing"* is described in a certain measure. It was a *"good thing toward Jehovah, the God of Israel."* The good thing looked towards the living God. In children there often will be found good things towards their parents. Let these be cultivated, but these are not sufficient evidences of grace. In children there will sometimes be found good things towards amiability and moral excellence. Let all good things be commended and fostered, but they are not sure fruits of grace.

It is toward God that the good thing must be that saves the soul. Remember how we read in the New Testament of repentance towards God and of faith in our Lord Jesus Christ. The way the face of the good thing looks is a main point about it. There is life in a look. If a man is traveling away from God, every step he takes increases his distance from Him. But if his face is toward the Lord, he may be only capable of a child's tottering step, but yet he is moving nearer and nearer every moment.

In Abijah was some good thing *"toward the Lord God,"* which is the most distinguishing mark of a truly good thing. The child had love, and there was in it love for Jehovah. He had faith, but it was faith in Jehovah. His religious fear was the fear of the living God. His child-like thoughts, desires, prayers, and hymns went towards the true God. This is what we desire to see not only in children, but in adults. We wish to see their hearts turned to the Lord, and their minds and wills moving towards the Most High.

In this dear child, that *"good thing"* worked such an outward character that he became exceedingly well-beloved. We are sure of that, because it is said *"all Israel shall mourn for him."* He was probably the heir to his father's crown, and there were godly but grieved hearts in Israel that hoped to see times of reform when that youth would come to the throne. Perhaps even those who did not care about religion, yet somehow had marked the youth as they had observed his going in and out before them, had said, "He is Israel's hope; there will be better days when that boy becomes a man." Thus when Abijah died, he alone of all his race received both tears and a tomb. He died lamented and was buried with respect, whereas all the rest of Jeroboam's house were devoured of dogs and vultures.

It is a very blessed thing when there is such a good thing in our children that they come to be beloved in their little spheres. They have not all the range which this young prince enjoyed so as to secure universal admiration. Still, the grace of God in a child is a very lovely thing, and it draws forth general approbation. Youthful piety is a very touching thing to me. I see the grace of God in men and women with much thankfulness, but I cannot perceive it in children without shedding tears of delight.

There is an exceeding beauty about these rosebuds of the Lord's garden. They have a fragrance which we find not in the fairest of earth's lilies. Love is won for the Lord Jesus in many a heart by these tiny arrows of the Lord, whose very smallness is a part of their power to penetrate the heart. The ungodly may not love the grace which is in the children, but since they love the children in whom that grace is found, they are no longer able to speak against religion as they otherwise would have done. Moreover, the Holy Spirit uses these children for yet higher ends, and those who see them are often impressed with desires for better things.

Chapter 21

More of "Some Good Thing"

And all Israel shall mourn for him, and bury him: for he only of Jeroboam shall come to the grave, because in him there is found some good thing toward the LORD God of Israel in the house of Jeroboam.
—1 Kings 14:13

He did not wear the broad phylactery. He had a meek and quiet spirit. He may not have been much of a speaker, or else it might have been said, "He has spoken good things concerning the God of Israel." He may have been a timid, retiring, almost silent boy, but the good thing was *"in him."* This is the kind of thing which we desire for every one of our friends, a work of grace within.

The grand point is not to wear the garb, nor use the brogue of religion, but to possess the life of God within, and feel and think as

Jesus would have done because of that inner life. Small is the value of external religion unless it is the outcome of a life within. True grace is not as a garment, to be put on and taken off, but it is an integral part of the person who possesses it. This child's piety was of the true, personal, inward kind. May all our children have some good thing in them!

We are told that this good thing *"was found"* in him: this means that it was discernible in him without much difficulty, for the expression *"found"* is used even when it does not imply any great search. Does not the Lord say, *"I am found of them that sought Me not"* (Isaiah 65:1)? Zealous, child-like piety soon shows itself. A child is usually far less reticent than a man. The little lip is not frozen by cold prudence, but reveals the heart. Godliness in a child appears even upon the surface, so that persons who come into the house as visitors are surprised by the artless statements which betray the young Christian.

There were many in Tirzah who could not help knowing that this child had in him some good thing towards Jehovah. They may not have cared to see it. They may have hoped it would be crushed out of him by the example of the court around him. Still they knew it was there—they had found it without difficulty.

Still, the expression does bear another shade of meaning: it implies that when God, the strict heart-searcher, who tries the reins of the children of men, visited this child, He found in him something for praise and glory: *"some good thing"* was discovered in him by those eyes which cannot be deceived. It is not all gold that glitters, but that which was in this child was genuine metal. Oh, that the like may be true of each of us when we are tried as by fire! It may be that his father was angry with him for serving Jehovah. But whatever his trial may have been, he came out of it unharmed.

The expression somewhat suggests to me the idea of surprise. How did this good thing get into the child? *"In him there is found some good thing,"* as when a man finds a treasure in a field. The farmer was thinking of nothing but his oxen, his acres, and his harvest, when all of a sudden his plow laid bare a hidden treasure. He found it where it was, but how it came to be there, he could not tell. So in this child, so disadvantageously placed, to the surprise of everybody, there was found *"some good thing toward the Lord God of Israel."* His conversion, you see, is veiled in mystery. About the grace in his heart, we are not told what it was, whence it came, nor what special actions it produced. Nevertheless, there it was, found where none expected it.

I believe that this case is typical of many of the elect children whom God calls by His grace in the courts and alleys of London. You must not expect that you will jot down their experiences, their feelings, and their lives, and total them all up. You must not reckon to know dates and means specifically, but you must take the child as we have to take Abijah, rejoicing to find in him a little wonder of grace with God's own seal upon him. The old prophet, in the name of the Lord, affirmed the young prince as a truehearted follower of the Most High. In like manner, the Lord sets His confirming mark of grace on regenerated children, and we must be content to see it, even if some other things are lacking. Let us welcome with delight those works of the Holy Spirit which we cannot precisely describe.

All that is said of this case was that there was in him *"some good thing."* This reads as if the divine work was as yet only a spark of grace, the beginning of spiritual life. There was nothing very striking in him, or it would be more definitely mentioned. He was not an heroic follower of Jehovah. His deeds of loyalty to God are not written, because by reason of his tender years he had neither power nor opportunity to do much which could be written. Inasmuch as we read that in him was *"some good thing,"* it is implied that it was not a perfect thing, and that it was not attended with all the good things one might wish for. Many good things were missing, but *"some good thing"* was manifest. Therefore the child was accepted and by divine love rescued from an ignoble death.

We are apt to overlook *"some good thing"* in a bad house. This was the most wonderful thing of all, that there should be a gracious child in Jeroboam's palace. The mother usually sways the house, but the queen was a princess of Egypt and an idolater. A father has great influence, but in this case Jeroboam sinned and made Israel to sin. It strikes me as a wonder that he should make Israel sin, but could not make his child sin. All the land feels the pestilent influence of Jeroboam, and yet close at his feet there is a bright spot which sovereign grace has kept from the plague. His firstborn, who naturally would imitate his father, is the very reverse of him—there is found in Jeroboam's heir *"some good thing toward the Lord God of Israel."* In such a place, we do not look for grace and are apt to pass it by.

If you go to the courts of our great cities, which are anything but palatial, you will see that they swarm with the children of the poor. You hardly expect to see grace where sin evidently abounds. In the fever dens and pestilent alleys of the great city, you hear blasphemy and see drunkenness on all sides, but do not therefore conclude that no child of God is there. Do not say within yourself, "The electing love of God has never aimed at any of these." How do you know? One of those poor little ragged children playing on a dust heap may have found Christ in the ragged school, and may be destined to a place at Christ's right hand. Precious is that gem, though cast amidst these pebbles. Bright is that diamond, though it lies upon a dunghill. If in the child there is *"some good thing toward the Lord God of Israel,"* he is none the less to be valued because his father is a thief and his mother is a gin drinker.

Never despise the most ragged child. A clergyman in Ireland, ministering to a little Protestant congregation, noticed for several Sundays, standing in the aisle near the door, a very tattered boy, who listened to the sermon most eagerly. He wished to know who the boy could be, but he always vanished as soon as the sermon was over. He asked a friend or two to watch, but somehow the boy always escaped and could not be discovered. It came to pass one Sunday that the minister preached a sermon from this text, *"His right hand, and His holy arm, hath gotten Him the victory"* (Psalm 98:1). After that time, he missed the boy altogether.

Six weeks elapsed, and the child did not come any more, but a man appeared from the hills and begged the minister to come and see his boy, who was dying. He lived in a miserable hovel up in the mountains. After a six-mile walk in the rain, through bogs and over hills, and the minister came to the door of the hut. As he entered, the poor lad was sitting up in bed. As soon as he caught sight of the preacher, the boy waved his arm and cried out, *"His right hand and His holy arm hath gotten Him the victory."* That was his closing speech on earth, his dying shout of triumph. Who knows but in many and many a case, the Lord's *"right hand and His holy arm have gotten Him the victory,"* despite the poverty and the sin and the ignorance that may have surrounded the young convert? Let us not therefore despise grace, wherever it is, but heartily prize what we are apt to overlook.

We cannot understand that God's dear little children, who love Him, should often be called to suffer. We say, "Well, if it were my child, I would heal him and ease his sufferings at once." Yet the Almighty Father allows His dear ones to be afflicted. The godly child of Jeroboam lies sick, and yet his wicked father is not sick, and his mother is not sick. We could almost wish they were, that they might do the less evil. Only one godly one is in the family, and he lies sick! Why was it so? Why is it so in other cases? You see a gracious child a cripple; you see a heavenly-minded girl a consumptive; you often see the heavy hand of God resting where His eternal love has fixed its choice. There is a meaning in all this, and we know somewhat of it. If we knew nothing, we would believe all the same in the goodness of the Lord.

Jeroboam's son was like the fig of the sycamore tree, which does not ripen until it is bruised: by his sickness, he was speedily ripened for glory. Besides, it was for his father's good and his mother's good that he was sick. If they had been willing to learn from the sorrow, it might have greatly blessed them. It did drive them to the prophet of God. Oh, that it had driven them to God Himself! A sick child has led many a blinded parent to the Savior, and eyes have thereby been opened.

There is something more remarkable still, and that is that some of God's dearest children die while they are yet young. I would have said let Jeroboam die and his wife also, but spare the child. But the child must go: he is the most fit. His departure was intended to give glory to God's grace in saving such a child, and making him so soon perfect. It was to be the reward of grace, for the child was taken from the evil to come. He was to die in peace and be buried, whereas the rest of the family would be slain with the sword and given to the jackals and the vultures to tear in pieces. In this child's case, his early death was a proof of grace.

If any say that converted children ought not to be taken into the church, I answer, "How is it the Lord takes so many of them into heaven? If they are fit for the one, they surely are fit for the other."

The Lord, in infinite mercy, often takes children home to Himself, saving them from the trials of long life and temptation; because not only is there grace in them, but there is so much more grace than usual that there is no need for delay. They are ripe already for the harvest. It is wonderful what great grace may dwell in a boy's heart. Child piety is by no means of an inferior kind. It is sometimes ripe for heaven.

Chapter 22

The Shunammite Woman's Son

Let me call your attention to an instructive miracle performed by the prophet Elisha, as recorded in the Second Book of Kings. The hospitality of the Shunammite woman had been rewarded by the gift of a son. But, alas! All earthly mercies are of uncertain tenure, and after a short number of years, the child fell sick and died.

The distressed but believing mother hastened at once to the man of God. Through him God had spoken the promise which fulfilled her heart's desire. She resolved to plead her case with him, so that he might lay it before his Divine Master and obtain for her an answer of peace. Elisha's action is recorded in the following verses:

> [29] *Then he said to Gehazi, Gird up thy loins, and take my staff in thine hand, and*

go thy way: if thou meet any man, salute him not, and if any salute thee, answer him not again: and lay my staff upon the face of the child.

[30] And the mother of the child said, As the Lord liveth, and as thy soul liveth, I will not leave thee. And he arose, and followed her.

[31] And Gehazi passed on before them, and laid the staff upon the face of the child; but there was neither voice, nor hearing. Wherefore he went again to meet him, and told him, saying, The child is not awaked.

[32] And when Elisha was come into the house, behold, the child was dead, and laid upon his bed.

[33] He went in therefore, and shut the door upon them twain, and prayed unto the Lord.

[34] And he went up, and lay upon the child, and put his mouth upon his mouth, and his eyes upon his eyes, and his hands upon his hands: and he stretched himself upon the child; and the flesh of the child waxed warm.

[35] Then he returned, and walked in the house to and fro; and went up, and stretched himself upon him: and the child sneezed seven times, and the child opened his eyes.

[36] And he called Gehazi, and said, Call this Shunammite. So he called her. And when she was come in unto him, he said, Take up thy son.

*37 Then she went in, and fell at his feet,
and bowed herself to the ground, and took
up her son and went out. (2 Kings 4:29-37)*

Elisha had to deal with a dead child. It is
true that, in his instance, it was natural death.
But the death with which you have to come in
contact is not the less real death because it is
spiritual. Boys and girls are as surely as grown-
up people, *"dead in trespasses and sins"*
(Ephesians 2:1). May none fail fully to realize
the state in which all human beings are naturally found. Unless you have a very clear sense
of the utter ruin and spiritual death of children, you will be incapable of being made a
blessing to them. Go to them, I pray you, not
as to sleepers whom you can by your own
power awaken from their slumber, but as to
spiritual corpses who can only be quickened by
a power divine.

Elisha **aimed at nothing less than the
restoration of the child to life**. May you
never be content with aiming at secondary
benefits, or even with realizing them. May you
strive for the grandest of all ends, the salvation
of immortal souls. Your business is not solely
to teach children to read the Bible, nor merely
to inculcate the duties of morality, nor even to
instruct them in the mere letter of the Gospel,
but your high calling is to be the means, in the
hands of God, of bringing life from heaven to
dead souls.

Resurrection, then, is our aim! To raise the dead is our mission! How is so strange a work to be achieved? If we yield to unbelief, we shall be staggered by the evident fact that the work to which the Lord has called us is quite beyond our own personal power. We cannot raise the dead. We are, however, no more powerless than Elisha, for he of himself could not restore the Shunammite's son. Need this fact discourage us? Does it not rather direct us to our true power by shutting us out from our own fancied might? I trust we are all of us already aware that the man who lives in the region of faith dwells in the realm of miracles.

Elisha was no common man now that God's Spirit was upon him, calling him to God's work, and aiding him in it. And you, devoted, anxious, prayerful teacher, remain no longer a common being. In a special manner, you have become the temple of the Holy Ghost. God dwells in you, and you by faith have entered upon the career of a wonder-worker. You are sent into the world not to do the things which are possible to man, but those impossibilities which the Holy Spirit works by means of believing people. You are to work miracles, to do marvels. You are not to look on the restoration of these dead children, which you are called to bring about, as being a thing unlikely or difficult when you remember who it is that works by your feeble instrumentality.

It would have been well if Elisha had recollected that he was once the servant of Elijah, and had so studied his master's example as to have imitated it. If so, he would not have sent Gehazi with a staff, but would have done at once what at last he was constrained to do. In 1 Kings 17, you will find the story of Elijah raising a dead child. You will there see that Elijah, the master, had left a complete model to his servant. It was not until Elisha followed that example in all respects that the miraculous power was manifested. It would had been wise if Elisha had, at the outset, imitated the pattern of the master whose mantle he wore.

With far more force, may I say to you that it will be well if, as teachers, we imitate the modes and methods of our glorified Master, and learn at His feet the art of winning souls. Just as He came in deepest sympathy into the nearest contact with our wretched humanity, and condescended to stoop to our sorrowful condition, so must we come near to the souls with whom we have to deal, yearn over them with His yearning, and weep over them with His tears, if we would see them raised from the state of sin. Only by imitating the spirit and manner of the Lord Jesus will we become wise to win souls.

I am afraid that very often the truth which we deliver is a thing which is extraneous and outside of ourselves. It is like a staff which we hold in our hand, but which is not a part of ourselves. We take doctrinal or practical truth, as Gehazi did the staff, and we lay it upon the face of the child. However, we ourselves do not agonize for its soul. We try this doctrine and that truth, this anecdote and another illustration, this way of teaching a lesson and that manner of delivering an address. Still, as long as the truth which we deliver is a matter apart from ourselves and unconnected with our innermost being, it will have no more effect upon a dead soul than Elisha's staff had upon the dead child.

We are not sure that Gehazi was convinced that the child was really dead. He spoke as if it were only asleep and needed waking. God will not bless those teachers who do not grasp in their hearts the really fallen estate of their children. If you think the child is not really depraved, if you indulge foolish notions about the innocence of childhood and the dignity of human nature, it should not surprise you if you remain barren and unfruitful.

Observe carefully what Elisha did when thus foiled in his first effort. When we fail in one attempt, we must not therefore give up our work. If you have been unsuccessful until now, you must not infer that you are not called to the work, any more than Elisha might have concluded that the child could not be restored.

The lesson of your lack of success is not to cease the work, but to change the method. It is not the person who is out of place, it is the plan which is unwise. If your first method has been unsuccessful, you must improve upon it. Examine where you have failed. Then, by changing your mode or spirit, the Lord may prepare you for a degree of usefulness far beyond your expectations. Elisha, instead of being dispirited when he found that the child was not awake, girded up his loins, and hastened with greater vigor to the work before him.

Chapter 23

Raising Children from the Dead

And when Elisha was come into the house, behold, the child was dead, and laid upon his bed. He went in therefore, and shut the door upon them twain, and prayed unto the LORD. And he went up, and lay upon the child, and put his mouth upon his mouth, and his eyes upon his eyes, and his hands upon his hands: and he stretched himself upon the child; and the flesh of the child waxed warm. Then he returned, and walked in the house to and fro; and went up, and stretched himself upon him: and the child sneezed seven times, and the child opened his eyes.
—2 Kings 4:32-35

N otice where the dead child was placed: "*And when Elisha was come into the house, behold, the child was dead, and laid upon his bed.*" This was the bed which the hospitality of the Shunammite had prepared for Elisha, the famous bed which, with the table, the stool, and the candlestick, will never be forgotten in the church of God.

In reading on we find, *"He went in, therefore, and shut the door upon them twain, and prayed unto the Lord."* Now the prophet is at his work in earnest, and we have a noble opportunity of learning from him the secret of raising children from the dead. If you turn to the narrative of Elijah in First Kings, you will find that Elisha adopted the orthodox method of proceeding—the method of his master Elijah. You will read there:

> [19] *And he said unto her, Give me thy son. And he took him out of her bosom, and carried him up into a loft, where he abode, and laid him upon his own bed.*
> [20] *And he cried unto the LORD, and said, O LORD, my God, hast thou also brought evil upon the widow with whom I sojourn, by slaying her son?*
> [21] *And he stretched himself upon the child three times, and cried unto the LORD, and said, O LORD, my God, I pray thee, let this child's soul come into him again.*
> [22] *And the LORD heard the voice of Elijah; and the soul of the child came into him again, and he revived.* (1 Kings 17:19-22)

The great secret lies in a large measure in powerful supplication. *"He shut the door upon them twain, and prayed unto the Lord."* An old proverb states, Every true pulpit is set up in heaven, by which is meant that the true preacher is much with God. If we do not pray to God for a blessing, if the foundation of the pulpit is not laid in private prayer, our open ministry will not be a success. So it is with you; every real teacher's power must come from on high. If you never enter your closet and shut to the door, if you never plead at the mercy seat for your child, how can you expect that God will honor you in the child's conversion?

It is a very excellent method, I think, actually to take the children one by one into your room alone and pray with them. You will see your children converted when God gives you to individualize their cases, to agonize for them, and to take them one by one, and to pray with them and for them with the door closed. There is much more influence in prayer privately offered with one than in prayer publicly uttered in the class—not more influence with God, of course, but more influence with the child. Such prayer will often be made its own answer: God may, while you are pouring out your soul, make your prayer to be the hammer to break the heart which mere talks had never touched.

After praying, Elisha adopted the means. Prayer and means must go together. **Means without prayer—presumption! Prayer without means—hypocrisy!**

There lay the child, and there stood the venerable man of God! Watch his extraordinary proceedings. He stoops over the corpse and puts his mouth upon the child's mouth. The cold, dead mouth of the child was touched by the warm, living lips of the prophet, and a vital stream of fresh, hot breath was sent down into the chill, stone-like passages of the dead mouth and throat and lungs. Next the holy man, with loving ardor of hopefulness, placed his eyes upon the child's eyes, and his hands upon the child's hands. The warm hands of the old man covered the cold palms of the departed child. Then he stretched himself upon the child and covered him with his whole body, as though he would transfer his own life into the lifeless frame, and would either die with him or would make him live.

We have heard of the chamois hunter acting as guide to a fearful traveler, who, when they came to a very dangerous part of the road, strapped the traveler firmly to himself and said, "Both of us or neither." That is to say, "Both of us shall live, or neither of us—we are one." So did the prophet effect a mysterious union between himself and the lad. In his own mind, it was resolved that he would either be chilled with the child's death, or warm the child with his life.

What does this teach us? The lessons are many and obvious. We see here, as in a picture, that if we would bring spiritual life to a child, we must most vividly realize that child's state. It is dead, dead. God will have you feel that the child is as dead in trespasses and sins as you once were. God would have you come into contact with that death by painful, crushing, humbling sympathy.

In soul winning, we should observe how our Master worked. Now, how did He work? When He would raise us from death, what was right for Him to do? He needed to die Himself: there was no other way. So it is with you. If you would raise that dead child, you must feel the chill and horror of that child's death yourself.

A dying man is needed to raise dying men. I cannot believe that you will ever pluck a brand from the burning, without putting your hand near enough to feel the heat of the fire. You must have, more or less, a distinct sense of the dreadful wrath of God and of the terrors of the judgment to come, or you will lack energy in your work, and so lack one of the essentials of success. I do not think the preacher ever speaks well upon such topics until he feels them pressing upon him as a personal burden from the Lord. "I did preach in chains," said John Bunyan, "to men in chains." Depend on it, when the death that is in your children alarms, depresses, and overwhelms you, then it is that God is about to bless you.

Thus realizing the child's state, and putting your mouth upon the child's mouth and your hands upon its hands, you must next strive to adapt yourself as far as possible to the nature, temperament, and habits of the child. Your mouth must find out the child's words, so that the child may know what you mean. You must see things with a child's eyes. Your heart must feel a child's feelings, so as to be his companion and friend. You must be a student of juvenile sin. You must be a sympathizer in juvenile trials. You must, so far as possible, enter into childhood's joys and griefs. You must not fret at the difficulty of this matter, or feel it to be humiliating. If anything difficult is required, you must do it, and not think it difficult. God will not raise a dead child by you if you are not willing to become all things to that child, that if by any possibility you may win its soul.

The prophet, *"stretched himself upon the child."* One would have thought it should be written "he contracted himself!" He was a full-grown man, and the other a mere lad. Should it not be "he contracted himself"? No, *"he stretched himself."* Mark you, no stretching is harder than for a man to stretch himself to a child. No fool is he who can talk to children. A simpleton is much mistaken if he thinks that his folly can interest boys and girls. It needs our best wits, our most industrious studies, our most earnest thoughts, our ripest powers, to teach our little ones. You will not quicken the child until you have *"stretched"* yourself. Though it seems a strange thing, yet it is so. The wisest man will need to exercise all his abilities if he would become a successful teacher of the young.

We see, then, in Elisha, a sense of the child's death and an adaptation of himself to his work. But above all, we see sympathy. While Elisha himself felt the chill of the corpse, his personal warmth was entering into the dead body. Of itself, this did not raise the child, but God worked through it. The old man's body heat passed into the child and became the medium of quickening.

Let every teacher weigh these words of Paul, *"But we were gentle among you, even as a nurse cherisheth her children: so being affectionately desirous of you, we were willing to have imparted unto you, not the gospel of God only, but also our own souls, because ye were dear unto us"* (1 Thessalonians 2:7-8). God will bless by His Spirit our heart's sympathy with His truth, and make it do that which the truth alone, coldly spoken, would not accomplish. Here, then, is the secret. You must impart to the young your own soul. You must feel as if the ruin of that child would be your own ruin.

The result of the prophet's work soon appeared, *"The flesh of the child waxed warm."*

How pleased Elisha must have been, but I do not find that his pleasure and satisfaction caused him to relax his exertions. Never be satisfied with finding your children in a barely hopeful state. What you want **is not mere conviction, but conversion**. You desire **not only impression, but regeneration**. Life from God, the life of Jesus—this your scholars need, and nothing less must content you.

"Then he returned, and walked in the house to and fro." Notice the restlessness of the man of God: he could not be easy. The child waxes warm (blessed be God for that), but he does not live yet. So, instead of sitting down by the table, the prophet walks to and fro with restless foot, disquieted, groaning, panting, longing, and ill at ease. He could not bear to look upon the disconsolate mother, or to hear her ask, "Is the child restored?" He continued pacing the house as if his body could not rest because his soul was not satisfied.

Imitate this **consecrated restlessness**. When you see a boy getting somewhat affected, do not sit down and say, "The child is very hopeful, thank God. I am perfectly satisfied." You will never win the priceless gem of a saved soul in that way. You must feel sad, restless, troubled, if you ever become a parent in the church.

After a short period of pacing, the prophet again *"went up and stretched himself upon the child."* What it is well to do once, it is proper to do a second time. What is good twice, is good seven times. There must be perseverance and patience. As surely as warmth went from Elisha to the child, so may cold go from you to your class unless you are in an earnest state of mind.

Elisha stretched himself on the bed again with many a prayer, many a sigh, and much believing. At last his desire was granted him: *"The child sneezed seven times, and the child opened his eyes."* Any form of action would indicate life and content the prophet. The child *"sneezed,"* some say, because he died with a disease of the head, for he said to his father, *"My head, my head!"* and the sneeze cleared the passages of life which had been blocked up. This we do not know. The fresh air entering afresh into the lungs might well compel a sneeze. The sound was nothing very articulate or musical, but it signified life.

This is all we should expect from young children when God gives them spiritual life. Some church members expect a great deal more, but for my part I am satisfied if the children sneeze—if they give any true sign of grace, however feeble or indistinct.

Perhaps if Gehazi had been there he would not have thought much of this sneezing, because he had never stretched himself upon the child, but Elisha was content with it. Even

189

so, if you and I have really agonized in prayer for souls, we will be very quick of eye to catch the first sign of grace, and will be thankful to God if the token be but a sneeze.

Then the child opened its eyes, and we will venture to say Elisha thought he had never seen such lovely eyes before. I know not what kind of eyes they were, the hazel or the blue, but this I know, that any eye which God helps you to open will be a beautiful eye to you.